New Day

Edited by Naomi Starkey　　　　　　　January–April 2015

New Daylight © BRF 2015

The Bible Reading Fellowship
15 The Chambers, Vineyard, Abingdon OX14 3FE
Tel: 01865 319700; Fax: 01865 319701
E-mail: enquiries@brf.org.uk; Website: www.brf.org.uk

ISBN 978 0 85746 122 3

Distributed in Australia by Mediacom Education Inc., PO Box 610, Unley, SA 5061.
Tel: 1800 811 311; Fax: 08 8297 8719;
E-mail: admin@mediacom.org.au
Available also from all good Christian bookshops in Australia.
For individual and group subscriptions in Australia:
Mrs Rosemary Morrall, PO Box W35, Wanniassa, ACT 2903.

Distributed in New Zealand by Scripture Union Wholesale, PO Box 760, Wellington
Tel: 04 385 0421; Fax: 04 384 3990; E-mail: suwholesale@clear.net.nz

Publications distributed to more than 60 countries

Acknowledgments
The New Revised Standard Version of the Bible, Anglicised Edition, copyright © 1989, 1995 by
the Division of Christian Education of the National Council of the Churches of Christ in the
USA. Used by permission. All rights reserved.

The Holy Bible, New International Version, Anglicised edition, copyright © 1979, 1984, 2011
by Biblica. Used by permission of Hodder & Stoughton Publishers, an Hachette UK company.
All rights reserved. 'NIV' is a registered trademark of Biblica. UK trademark number 1448790.

Scripture quotations marked (GNB) are from the Good News Bible published by The Bible
Societies/HarperCollins Publishers, copyright © 1966, 1971, 1976, 1992 American Bible
Society.

Extracts from the Authorised Version of the Bible (The King James Bible), the rights in which
are vested in the Crown, are reproduced by permission of the Crown's Patentee, Cambridge
University Press.

Scripture quotations from the Contemporary English Version © American Bible Society 1991,
1992, 1995. Used by permission/Anglications © British and Foreign Bible Society 1997.

Scripture quotations marked (NLT) are taken from the Holy Bible, New Living Translation,
copyright © 1996, 2004. Used by permission of Tyndale House Publishers, Inc., Wheaton,
Illinois 60189. All rights reserved.

Easy-to-Read Version (ERV) copyright ©2006 World Bible Translation Center.

The New Testament in Modern English, Revised Edition, translated by J.B. Phillips. Published by
HarperCollins Publishers Ltd. Copyright © 1958, 1960, 1972 by J.B. Phillips.

Extracts from The Book of Common Prayer of 1662, the rights of which are vested in the
Crown in perpetuity within the United Kingdom, are reproduced by permission of Cambridge
University Press, Her Majesty's Printers.

The Revised Common Lectionary is copyright © The Consultation on Common Texts, 1992 and is
reproduced with permission. *The Christian Year: Calendar, Lectionary and Collects*, which includes
the *Common Worship* lectionary (the Church of England's adaptations of the *Revised Common
Lectionary*, published as the Principal Service lectionary) is copyright © The Central Board of
Finance of the Church of England, 1995, 1997, and material from it is reproduced with
permission.

Printed by Gutenberg Press, Tarxien, Malta.

Suggestions for using New Daylight

Find a regular time and place, if possible, where you can read and pray undisturbed. Before you begin, take time to be still and perhaps use the BRF prayer. Then read the Bible passage slowly (try reading it aloud if you find it over-familiar), followed by the comment. You can also use New Daylight for group study and discussion, if you prefer.

The prayer or point for reflection can be a starting point for your own meditation and prayer. Many people like to keep a journal to record their thoughts about a Bible passage and items for prayer. In New Daylight we also note the Sundays and some special festivals from the Church calendar, to keep in step with the Christian year.

New Daylight and the Bible

New Daylight contributors use a range of Bible versions, and you will find a list of the versions used opposite, on page 2. You are welcome to use your own preferred version alongside the passage printed in the notes. This can be particularly helpful if the Bible text has been abridged.

New Daylight affirms that the whole of the Bible is God's revelation to us, and we should read, reflect on and learn from every part of both Old and New Testaments. Usually the printed comment presents a straight-forward 'thought for the day', but sometimes it may also raise questions rather than simply providing answers, as we wrestle with some of the more difficult passages of Scripture.

New Daylight is also available in a deluxe edition (larger format). Visit your local Christian bookshop or contact the BRF office, who can also give details about a cassette version for the visually impaired. For a Braille edition, contact St John's Guild, 8 St Raphael's Court, Avenue Road, St Albans, AL1 3EH.

Comment on New Daylight

To send feedback, you may email or write to BRF at the addresses shown opposite. If you would like your comment to be included on our website, please email connect@brf.org.uk. You can also Tweet to @brfonline, using the hashtag #brfconnect.

Writers in this issue

Stephen Rand is an activist, writer and speaker who worked with Tearfund for many years, and then Open Doors, travelling widely. He now helps to lead Fresh Streams, a largely Baptist church leaders' network. He and his wife Susan live in Oxfordshire.

Stephen Cottrell is the Bishop of Chelmsford. He has worked as Missioner in the Wakefield diocese and as part of Springboard, the Archbishop's evangelism team. His latest books are *From the Abundance of the Heart* (DLT, 2006) and *Do Nothing to Change Your Life* (CHP, 2007).

Andy John has been the Bishop of Bangor since 2008, having previously served all his ministry in the Diocese of St Davids. He is married to Caroline, who is a deacon in the Church in Wales.

Rachel Boulding is Deputy Editor of the *Church Times*. Before this, she was Senior Editor at SPCK Publishing, and then Senior Liturgy Editor at Church House Publishing. She lives in Dorset with her husband and son—and, during school terms, more than 70 teenage boys.

Lakshmi Jeffreys, as an Anglican priest, has served in parish ministry, university chaplaincy and as a mission officer across a diocese. She is involved in church leadership in a village just outside Northampton.

Penelope Wilcock writes Christian fiction, pastoral theology and Bible study. Her books include 'The Hawk & the Dove' series, *Spiritual Care of Dying and Bereaved People*, *100 Stand-Alone Bible Studies* and *Learning To Let Go*. She blogs at http://kindredofthequietway.blogspot.co.uk.

David Runcorn is a writer, spiritual director, theological teacher, retreat leader and conference speaker. He lives in Gloucester. You can meet him at www.davidruncorn.com.

Naomi Starkey is a Commissioning Editor for BRF and edits and writes for *New Daylight* Bible reading notes. She has also written *The Recovery of Love* (BRF, 2012).

Barbara Mosse is a retired Anglican priest with experience in various chaplaincies. A freelance lecturer and retreat giver, she is the author of *Encircling the Christian Year* (BRF. 2012) and *Welcoming the Way of the Cross* (BRF, 2013).

John Twisleton is parish priest of Horsted Keynes in West Sussex. He is the author of *Meet Jesus* (BRF, 2011) and *Using the Jesus Prayer* (BRF, 2014) and broadcasts regularly on Premier Christian Radio.

Naomi Starkey writes...

As I have continued my theological studies, I have been struck by the greater awareness these days of the various ways in which different people absorb and process information—and how important it is that those involved in preaching and teaching are aware of these differences.

In the past, education was synonymous with 'book-learning' and, if you struggled with reading (through undiagnosed dyslexia, for example), there was often little sympathy and too much readiness to throw around disparaging labels. Those training to be teachers today (so a friend tells me) not only have to be aware of different learning styles but use a range of skills to help all learners gain maximum benefit from their lessons.

Down the centuries, the church has, in fact, been very good at using a variety of ways to teach people the Christian faith. Medieval churches were places of vibrant imagery and colour, designed to teach biblical truths to largely illiterate congregations. More recently, the Methodist Church, among others, has been noted for using hymns to convey theological teaching. Sing an exquisitely crafted Charles Wesley hymn and by the end you feel as if you have done a full evening's Bible study! The growing popularity of *lectio divina*, meditating on scripture using the 'eyes of the heart', has encouraged people to use their imagination to make connections with what they are reading. Meanwhile, the use of icons to aid devotion has spread far beyond the Orthodox Church.

Bearing all that in mind, in this issue of *New Daylight* we are including a couple of new approaches to daily Bible reading. The first involves focusing in some detail on selected chapters in John's Gospel. That Gospel is perhaps deeper and more densely textured than any other and richly rewards slow and considered reflection. The second approach involves taking a well-known, well-loved hymn (in this instance, Rachel Boulding focuses on 'Dear Lord and Father of mankind') and exploring the theology behind it, linked to relevant Bible passages.

The aim, as always, is to help you engage with the Bible (even with the most familiar passages) in ways that encourage you in your walk of faith, day by day—whatever your preferred learning style.

The BRF Prayer

Almighty God,
you have taught us that your word is a lamp for our feet
and a light for our path. Help us, and all who prayerfully
read your word, to deepen our fellowship with you
and with each other through your love.
And in so doing may we come to know you more fully,
love you more truly, and follow more faithfully
in the steps of your son Jesus Christ, who lives and reigns
with you and the Holy Spirit, one God for evermore.
Amen

'Your law gives me delight'

Welcome to 2015! Whether or not you are bleary-eyed after seeing in the New Year, note the heading for the following series of passages: 'Your law gives me delight'.

If you have ever opened your Bible and dipped into Leviticus or Deuteronomy, you may have found it difficult to believe that anyone could say, 'Your law gives me delight', but the writer of Psalm 119 said it—and this is verse 174 of his poem of delight. Every verse has a word to describe the law: decrees, precepts, commands, word, promise; it is as if a brilliant diamond is being turned so that every facet can sparkle.

Part of our difficulty today is that we are victims of translation. First, we have traditionally used the word 'Law' for the Hebrew 'Torah'—the word used to describe Jewish religious teaching. Torah appears 219 times in the Old Testament and every time the King James Version translates it as 'law', but 'Torah' is a richer word than that. It could be translated as 'teaching', 'instruction' or 'guidance'. I find it easier to imagine myself delighting in God's 'guidance': it is just what I need at the start of the year!

Of course, to many, the 'law' in a biblical context means the ten commandments. Again, there is a translation issue. The word translated as 'commandments' is common in the Old Testament and most commonly translated elsewhere as 'words'. One of the greatest delights in life is the discovery that God has spoken.

I remember being told a story—quite probably apocryphal—of a man walking into an historic parish church and seeing a woman quietly staring at the ancient boards either side of the altar. 'I see you are studying the ten commandments', he said. 'Is that what they are?' she replied. 'I thought they were ten promises.' She saw not a list of onerous demands that together made a heavy burden, but, rather, the hope of a life transformed by the presence and the power of God by his Spirit.

So, are you ready? You are invited to start the year by exploring the law—shining a light on God's words, God's guidance, God's promises—and, as the facets of the diamond sparkle, my prayer is that you will be given a new delight.

Stephen Rand

Remember... walk in his ways

Remember how the Lord your God led you all the way in the wilderness these forty years... feeding you with manna, which neither you nor your ancestors had known, to teach you that man does not live on bread alone but on every word that comes from the mouth of the Lord... Observe the commands of the Lord your God, walking in obedience to him and revering him. For the Lord your God is bringing you into a good land... a land where bread will not be scarce and you will lack nothing... When you have eaten and are satisfied, praise the Lord your God for the good land he has given you. Be careful that you do not forget the Lord your God, failing to observe his commands.

The New Year provides us with an opportunity to look back and to look ahead. As the Israelites stood on the verge of a new start in a new land, Moses did the same. He looked back over 40 years of what we sometimes call 'wandering in the wilderness'.

He remembered it as a time when they had been led by God and God had provided for them. He had given them their daily bread, but their dependency on God—and his faithfulness in meeting their needs—went much further. Their lives—and our lives as well—were and are entirely dependent on God, physically, materially and spiritually.

'Every word that comes from the mouth of the Lord' (v. 3) includes God's promises, God's covenant... and his commandments. Deuteronomy 8:18 reinforces the point: 'Remember the Lord your God, for it is he who gives you the ability to produce wealth, and so confirms his covenant...'

They could look back and remember and, thus, look ahead with confidence, providing they continued to walk in obedience to God. The Hebrew in verse 6 can be translated as 'walk in his ways'. That is what followers do. If obeying the law sounds like a heavy burden, take delight that, in 2015, you are being asked to walk with the Lord.

Reflection

Start the year as you mean to go on—remember the Lord your God and walk in his ways.

STEPHEN RAND

Radiant

Moses was there with the Lord forty days and forty nights without eating bread or drinking water. And he wrote on the tablets the words of the covenant—the Ten Commandments. When Moses came down from Mount Sinai with the two tablets of the covenant law in his hands, he was not aware that his face was radiant because he had spoken with the Lord. When Aaron and all the Israelites saw Moses, his face was radiant, and they were afraid to come near him.

'Tablets of stone' sound hard—perhaps even hard to swallow! Today's passage reminds us that the law was given in the context of Moses' personal experience of God. It came out of relationship.

For 40 days and 40 nights Moses was with the Lord, an experience so intense that he did not need physical sustenance. The passage gives a strong hint that the experience was a conversation: 'he had spoken with the Lord' (v. 29). This was not like being summoned to the head-teacher's office for instructions to be issued; rather, it was a lengthy discussion about the nature of their relationship, what it would mean to 'walk in his ways'. The result was a covenant, a promise, and it was all summed up in ten words: verse 28 could be translated, 'He wrote on the tablets the words of the covenant, the ten words.' We now call them the ten commandments.

So, how was Moses after this 40-day fast spent in conversation with God? When Aaron and the people saw him, he did not look exhausted or emaciated, he looked radiant. They could tell just by looking at him that he had been with God. His face reflected God's light, God's glory.

So many people look at Christians and see faces (and lives) more like the tablets of stone than reflecting the radiance of Christ's presence. What do you want most in this New Year? In my better moments, I long to know God so that my experience of him lights up the lives of all those I meet.

Prayer

Gracious Father, help me to spend time with you, to speak with you and to hear you speak, so that, as I walk with you, my life is filled with your radiance. Amen

STEPHEN RAND

The law of love

Moses chiselled out two stone tablets like the first ones and went up Mount Sinai early in the morning, as the Lord had commanded him... Then the Lord came down in the cloud and stood there with him... proclaiming, 'The Lord, the Lord, the compassionate and gracious God, slow to anger, abounding in love and faithfulness, maintaining love to thousands, and forgiving wickedness, rebellion and sin. Yet he does not leave the guilty unpunished; he punishes the children and their children for the sin of the parents to the third and fourth generation.' Moses bowed to the ground at once and worshipped.

Laws reflect the values of those who make them. I once belonged to a church that demanded 2s/6d from anyone wishing to play the organ— despite many years having passed since decimal coinage had been introduced! Just a hint of a church lagging painfully behind the times?

Moses has returned to meet with God after smashing the first tablets when he discovered that the Israelites had worshipped a golden calf in his absence. He has pleaded with God for the people; he has also pleaded that God should continue to teach him and go with him. He asks for an even greater revelation from God. His longing is rewarded. God reveals himself, and then the stone tablets are reissued. This time they are introduced by the name and description of the one who is initiating this covenant and delivering his guidance as to how human beings, created in his image, should live.

First, his name is repeated—perhaps a reminder that it encapsulates his nature and character. Next he is defined as 'compassionate and gracious... abounding in love' (v. 6). It is nonsense to suggest that the New Testament reveals a God of love who has somehow changed his nature from that revealed in the Old Testament. God is consistent and unchangeable. His holiness and consistency means guilt has to be punished; but the starting point is compassion, grace, faithfulness and love. This is the context in which we can delight in the law: it stems from a God who is abounding in love. No wonder Moses worshipped!

Prayer

Almighty God, thank you for the evidence of your love and grace to me.

Stephen Rand

The God who speaks, acts and frees

And God spoke all these words: 'I am the Lord your God, who brought you out of Egypt, out of the land of slavery. You shall have no other gods before me.'

As you may have noticed, if you start reading the Bible at Genesis 1, a lot happens before you reach Exodus 20! God creates, people sin, God chooses, God promises, God sets his people free.

God created by means of his words: 'He spoke, and it came to be' (Psalm 33:9). He spoke to Moses from a burning bush and the liberation of his people from slavery in Egypt began. God does not deal in idle words. So, the presentation of the law begins with God speaking. He gives his name. Then he gives one outstanding credential: 'who brought you… out of the land of slavery' (v. 2).

The law, then, is not given by a distant God. His guidance, his directions, his commands do not come out of a vacuum. They arrive as part of a story: a story of relationship, love, freedom, redemption. God's words and his actions are inseparable from his character. He is able to demand and expect the sole and focused worship of his people because he has created them, loved them and saved them.

Until this moment in history, there was no written record of God, no scriptures. They knew what God was like because of their experience of what he had done. They had seen him in action.

You are more likely to use a recipe book after you have tasted the food its author has made; a budding athlete would take Mo Farah's guide to becoming a world champion rather more seriously than anything I could write, especially if they had seen me running for a bus.

God is God. He could simply demand our worship and our obedience, but, because God is God, he acts in love and mercy on our behalf and, thus, earns and reinforces his right to receive our praise and our lives lived under the guidance of his law.

Reflection

'Tell the heavens and the earth to start singing!… The Lord has rescued his people; now they will worship him' (Isaiah 44:23, CEV).

Stephen Rand

Representing God to the world

See, I have taught you decrees and laws as the Lord my God commanded me, so that you may follow them in the land you are
entering to take possession of it. Observe them carefully, for this
will show your wisdom and understanding to the nations, who will
hear about all these decrees and say, 'Surely this great nation is
a wise and understanding people.' What other nation is so great
as to have their gods near them the way the Lord our God is near
us whenever we pray to him? And what other nation is so great as
to have such righteous decrees and laws as this body of laws I am
setting before you today?

As Moses prepares to receive the ten commandments, God says: 'Now
if you obey me fully and keep my covenant, then out of all nations you
will be my treasured possession… a kingdom of priests and a holy
nation' (Exodus 19:5–6). God's people were not chosen because they
were better than others, nor special in themselves. They were chosen to
know God and represent him to the world. They were to live in the
world and before the world in such a way that they would show what
God was like and commend him to the nations.

This has always been God's way. His love and blessings are to be
shared and multiplied. Key to fulfilling that purpose is obedience, demonstrating what it means to live in relationship with God.

Most adults who become Christians begin their journey to faith by
observing someone whose life has been changed for the better by knowing Jesus. Thus, when God's people fail to live in God's way, they not
only spoil their relationship with God but also compromise God's mission. The behaviour of the church and individual Christians can
undoubtedly be a barrier for many people searching for God.

It is said that Gandhi was asked how Christianity might become part
of the national life of India. Gandhi responded: 'First, I would suggest
all of you Christians must begin to live more like Jesus Christ.'

Prayer

*Dear Lord, help me to live my life so that it demonstrates your love and
draws others to you.*

STEPHEN RAND

DEUTERONOMY 10:12–13 (NRSV)

Fear, walk, love, serve, obey

So now, O Israel, what does the Lord your God require of you? Only to fear the Lord your God, to walk in all his ways, to love him, to serve the Lord your God with all your heart and with all your soul, and to keep the commandments of the Lord your God and his decrees that I am commanding you today, for your own well-being.

This is a succinct summary of the whole revelation of God given in the law of Moses, the first five books of the Bible, from the perspective of human beings. If God has made us in his image, what does he expect from us in return?

First, we are to fear God. Surely, though, God is our father, friend, saviour. Why should we fear him? It cannot mean we should be frightened of him. While the Hebrew word translated as 'fear' can mean 'to revere' or 'respect', this does not entirely capture it either. The best analogy I can suggest is that, having lived in a loving relationship with Susan for more than 40 years, she shapes my behaviour. I love to do what pleases her, to make her happy. I fear, almost more than anything, that I will do something to destroy our relationship. William D. Eisenhower, an American Presbyterian minister, said, 'Fear of the Lord is the beginning of wisdom, but love from the Lord is its completion.'

Second, we are 'to walk in all his ways' (v. 12). Keep moving forward, in step with his Spirit, arm-in-arm, while following his guidance and direction.

Next, we are to love and serve him. Again, the analogy of marriage helps us here. Love is not just an emotion, nor even just a word we say (though many do not say it often enough!) It is also a prompt to action. If we love God, we will do what he wants and, as we shall see, we serve him by serving others: 'The truth is, anything you did for any of my people here, you also did for me' (Matthew 25:40, ERV).

Reflection

God's promise is that if we fear, walk, love, serve and obey, it will be for our own 'well-being'. God's way is the best way to live!

STEPHEN RAND

Orphans, widows and foreigners

For the Lord your God is God of gods and Lord of lords, the great God, mighty and awesome, who shows no partiality and accepts no bribes. He defends the cause of the fatherless and the widow, and loves the foreigner residing among you, giving them food and clothing. And you are to love those who are foreigners, for you yourselves were foreigners in Egypt.

The character of God the lawgiver is revealed further by this summary. Clearly, the law is rooted in the expectation that the behaviour of God's people will reflect his character. 'You must be perfect, just as your Father in heaven is perfect', said Jesus (Matthew 5:48, ERV). Another translation is worded, 'But you must always act like your Father in heaven' (CEV). The more we get to know God, the more we will understand how to live.

First, God 'shows no partiality' (v. 17); all human beings are made in the image of God, so all are treated equally. Favouritism is not only wrong but also potentially destructive, whether in a family, church or community. Neither can God be bought; he 'accepts no bribes' (v. 17). All through the law, there is an oft-repeated insistence that public justice must not be corrupted by wealth, but must be equally available to rich and poor. The law is concerned with public law as well as personal morality; with the nation, the community, the family and the individual.

God 'defends the cause of the fatherless and the widow, and loves the foreigner' (v. 18). What do these three groups have in common and why does the law so clearly demand their protection and support? It is because the land was shared out equally between each family of God's people and passed down through the male line. The fatherless, the widow and the foreigner had two things in common: first, they had no direct access to the land and therefore the food it produced; second, their well-being was the communal responsibility of the people of God. It still is.

Prayer

Almighty God, you are a father to the fatherless, defender of widows; you place the lonely in families. Grant your church the wisdom and courage to be and do the same. (Based on Psalm 68:5–6.)

STEPHEN RAND

DEUTERONOMY 15:4–11 (NIV, ABRIDGED)

Open-handed, not tight-fisted

However, there need be no poor people among you, for in the land the Lord your God is giving you to possess as your inheritance, he will richly bless you, if only you fully obey the Lord your God... If anyone is poor among your fellow Israelites in any of the towns of the land that the Lord your God is giving you, do not be hard-hearted or tight-fisted towards them. Rather, be open-handed... Give generously to them and do so without a grudging heart... There will always be poor people in the land. Therefore I command you to be open-handed towards your fellow Israelites who are poor and needy in your land.

Does the Bible contradict itself? The verses above say there need be 'no poor people among you' but also that 'there will always be poor people'! In the past I have even had a minister quote those words as a justification for not supporting a Tearfund project to help poor people.

This demonstrates the importance of reading Bible verses in context and making sure we understand the original meaning. The first verse above actually makes it clear that if the people 'fully obey', then there will be no poor people. The law had detailed proposals designed to help those who were poor, not least cancelling debt and giving people a new start, as well as these instructions to be open-handed rather than tight-fisted.

So, the final verse above is recognition that people would not 'fully obey' and, therefore, there would still be those desperate for a habitable home, a decent meal. It is definitely not a 'get-out' clause, though, enabling people to imagine that they can 'pass by on the other side'. No! The verse is emphatic: the continuing presence of poor people in our society will require us once again to be open-handed. The law of generous giving is not annulled; rather, there will be plenty of opportunities for it to be put into action.

Reflection

The law was good news to the poor; Jesus was good news to the poor. Thus, the gospel is good news to the poor. How much, though, is the church, your church, good news to the poor?

STEPHEN RAND

LEVITICUS 25:1–5, 14, 23–24 (NIV, ABRIDGED)

The law of the land

The Lord said to Moses at Mount Sinai, 'Speak to the Israelites and say to them: "When you enter the land I am going to give you, the land itself must observe a sabbath to the Lord... Do not sow your fields or prune your vineyards... The land is to have a year of rest... If you sell land to any of your own people or buy land from them, do not take advantage of each other... The land must not be sold permanently, because the land is mine and you reside in my land as foreigners and strangers. Throughout the land that you hold as a possession, you must provide for the redemption of the land."'

The law given to Moses includes enormous detail about how the people of God should live in the land and on the land. Though it may at first seem irrelevant to us, this detail is an outworking of some basic principles that are, I believe, vitally relevant to our understanding of how God wants us to live now, some 4000 years later.

The first principle is that the land belongs to God: 'To the Lord your God belong the heavens, even the highest heavens, the earth and everything in it' (Deuteronomy 10:14). It is because it belongs to God that he is able to give it to the Israelites and also insist that it cannot be sold permanently.

The second principle is that people are tenants, not owners, of the land: they 'hold [it] as a possession' (v. 24). In the creation narrative, Adam is instructed by God to 'take care' of the land (Genesis 2:15). In today's passage, that care extends to managing it sensitively—giving it a year of rest—and not exploiting it or other tenants of it – 'do not take advantage of each other' (v. 14).

Third, obedience requires trust. A farmer who does not sow for one year is trusting God to provide food in that sabbath year. Every mouthful of food we eat is a reminder of God's grace and provision.

Reflection

The earth is the Lord's: he made it, he sustains it, he will redeem it, he asks us to take care of it. Christians should be the most enthusiastic environmentalists in the world.

STEPHEN RAND

A new covenant

'The days are coming... when I will make a new covenant... because they broke my covenant, though I was a husband to them,' declares the Lord... 'I will put my law in their minds and write it on their hearts. I will be their God, and they will be my people. No longer will they teach their neighbour, or say to one another, "Know the Lord," because they will all know me, from the least of them to the greatest,' declares the Lord. 'For I will forgive their wickedness and will remember their sins no more.'

By this time, over 1000 years had passed since the law had been given to Moses, but we see here that the people failed to keep it. This failure began when a golden calf was made even while Moses was up the mountain with God and, despite some brief exceptions, sin and rebellion led to their exile. God has not given up yet, though.

The people broke their side of the covenant. What does God do? He picks up the pieces and reconstructs it. The core is unchanged: 'I will be their God, and they will be my people' (v. 33). The content is the same: 'my law'. It is still God's initiative; it is still a promise of relationship.

So how is it different? The old covenant was written on tablets of stone, but now it will be written on their hearts. It will not only be integral to their intellect but also their emotions. Even this is not different, however—more intensely stated, perhaps, but not different.

Here is a clue to the answer: the phrase 'new covenant' is not repeated until Luke 22:20, when Jesus presides at the Last Supper and says, 'This cup is the new covenant in my blood, which is poured out for you.' The next day, Jesus' blood was poured out on the cross and the temple curtain that sealed off the Holy of Holies was torn apart. The death of Jesus made it possible for all—from the least to the greatest—to know forgiveness and come into God's presence. There was no longer a barrier, no longer a human mediator required.

Prayer

Dear God, thank you that my sins can be forgiven and forgotten and I can know you.

STEPHEN RAND

Dying to the law, living to God

A person is not justified by the works of the law, but by faith in Jesus Christ… For through the law I died to the law so that I might live for God. I have been crucified with Christ and I no longer live, but Christ lives in me. The life I now live in the body, I live by faith in the Son of God, who loved me and gave himself for me. I do not set aside the grace of God, for if righteousness could be gained through the law, Christ died for nothing!

Paul had grown up steeped in the Law. He had studied it, it was his special subject. Here he is writing to the Galatians, who were not Jews, but still wrestling with what to them was a vital question: did following Jesus mean that they had to observe the full range of the Jewish Law? They had received visitors who insisted that they did. This provoked Paul into almost a righteous rage. He had been through this before, arguing ferociously with Peter, whom he had opposed to his face. In today's passage, Paul is quoting what he had said to Peter.

His argument is that his relationship with God and his assurance of being with God now and into eternity is entirely based on his faith in Jesus who had died. The Law made it clear that he could not be with God because he could not keep the Law in its entirety—but Jesus did! So, Paul goes on to write, 'Christ redeemed us from the curse of the law by becoming a curse for us' (3:13). He believed passionately that his only hope—everyone's only hope—was to identify with Jesus, to be 'crucified with Christ' so that 'Christ lives in me' (v. 20).

Jesus fulfilled the Law in two ways: he lived by it and gives his Spirit to those who cannot live by it: 'He redeemed us in order that the blessing given to Abraham might come to the Gentiles through Christ Jesus, so that by faith we might receive the promise of the Spirit' (v. 14).

Prayer

Loving Father, help me to live by faith, because Christ lives in me.

STEPHEN RAND

MATTHEW 5:17–20 (NIV, ABRIDGED)

Fulfilment

'Do not think that I have come to abolish the Law or the Prophets; I have not come to abolish them but to fulfil them. For truly I tell you, until heaven and earth disappear, not the smallest letter, not the least stroke of a pen, will by any means disappear from the Law until everything is accomplished. Therefore… whoever practises and teaches these commands will be called great in the kingdom of heaven. For I tell you that unless your righteousness surpasses that of the Pharisees and the teachers of the Law, you will certainly not enter the kingdom of heaven.'

I wonder if anyone in the Galatian church read Paul's letter (see yesterday's notes) and wrote back, 'So what did Jesus mean in the Sermon on the Mount?' There was one obvious point of agreement—Jesus fulfilled the Law—but Paul appeared to be saying that the Law no longer had to be observed, while Jesus was emphasising that not one bit of it should be ignored.

Part of the answer lies in the context of the two passages. Jesus was faced with the scribes (teachers of the Law), dedicated to defining its principles in the minutiae of everyday life, and the Pharisees, who had separated themselves from all risk of defilement while they observed every detail the scribes could offer them.

Jesus' ministry collides with these two groups. To them, he does not take the Law seriously: he heals on the sabbath; he ignores ritual purity. Jesus responds by indicating that they are missing the point: the Law is not about external ritual observance, but real behaviour that stems from internal attitudes. He sets an even higher standard.

It was—and is—a standard that cannot be reached by us. Jesus fulfilled the Law by living his life according to that standard. Although keeping the Law was beyond us, it was not beyond him and he has made it possible for us to share his life by faith, so that we can enter the kingdom of heaven.

Reflection

'No one comes to the Father except through me' (John 14:6). It is because Jesus fulfilled the law in his life and his death that he is the only way to God.

STEPHEN RAND

The most important commandment

One of the teachers of the law came and heard them debating. Noticing that Jesus had given them a good answer, he asked him, 'Of all the commandments, which is the most important?' 'The most important one,' answered Jesus, 'is this: "Hear, O Israel: the Lord our God, the Lord is one. Love the Lord your God with all your heart and with all your soul and with all your mind and with all your strength." The second is this: "Love your neighbour as yourself." There is no commandment greater than these.'

We love lists—I even have a book of them! On holiday, I often use those travel guides that list the top ten places to go and things to see. Just a few days ago, people were wondering what song would be the Christmas number one. So here, a teacher of the Law comes with what may be a trick question: the Law is full of commandments, but which is the most important? I cannot quite help feeling that Jesus gives almost a politician's answer. He is asked for one… and he gives two!

I think the translation here works against us understanding the full implication of what Jesus says. The question is, 'Of all the commandments, which is the first?' Not unreasonably, the translation turns this into, 'which is the most important?' So, when Jesus says, 'The first is…', once again it is translated as, 'The most important one', which makes good sense because surely nothing is more important than to love God?

Jesus does not have just one on his list, though. There is a second. One little Greek word is not translated here, but it is in the King James Version: 'And the second is like, namely this…' 'Like' means that it resembles it, is the same as it. One translation does capture this exactly: 'The second is equally important…' (NLT).

The story of religion is all about people trying to find ways to love God that are focused on ritual observance but do not really affect their attitudes and behaviour. Here, though, the message is clear: you need to follow two commandments as you cannot love God without loving your neighbour.

Reflection

'Therefore love is the fulfilment of the law' (Romans 13:10).

STEPHEN RAND

More precious than gold

The law of the Lord is perfect, refreshing the soul. The statutes of the Lord are trustworthy, making wise the simple. The precepts of the Lord are right, giving joy to the heart. The commands of the Lord are radiant, giving light to the eyes. The fear of the Lord is pure, enduring for ever. The decrees of the Lord are firm, and all of them are righteous. They are more precious than gold, than much pure gold; they are sweeter than honey, than honey from the honeycomb.

I almost feel that any comment here is superfluous! Please read these beautiful verses again, asking God to use his word to refresh your soul. Then take in the wonderful range of adjectives used to describe God's word: perfect, refreshing, trustworthy, right, joy-giving, radiant, light-giving, firm, precious and sweet. Are you looking for refreshment, for wisdom, for light, for joy? These all come from God as he reveals himself in his word through his Spirit.

Our culture is dominated by the search for wealth. Gold is seen as one of the safest investments. How much more wealth could we hope to receive than the return on time spent investing in exploring God's teachings and getting to know God himself.

Our culture, too, is focused on food. I have tasted honey straight from the honeycomb, cut especially for me from the top of a palm tree near the beach in Sri Lanka. It tasted good! In Psalm 34:8, we are encouraged to 'taste and see that the Lord is good'. If we seek God in his word, we will discover just how sweet spending time with God can be.

This is not an appeal to become super-spiritual or focus on biblical meditation so much that we withdraw from engaging with the world. Rather, it is the recognition of an activist, which is that if I am to change the world and build God's kingdom, then I need to be constantly refreshed and reignited with God's passion and love by encountering him powerfully in and through his word. Then we can live in God's world God's way. Life does not come any better than that!

Prayer

'Open my eyes, that I may see wonderful things in your law'
(Psalm 119:18).

STEPHEN RAND

John 6: Living bread

I do not know how many times I have preached on this passage. John 6 is one of my favourite bits of the Bible, so, when I was invited to write these notes, I jumped at the chance of going into the story in greater detail.

When preaching, I usually juxtapose the beginning and end of the chapter. It starts, as you will discover, with a small boy and his lunch box and Jesus feeding the crowds, but ends with disappointment—all the crowds depart and Jesus is left alone with his few disciples.

Why this turnaround? Well, the crowd that got the free lunch on day one comes back for another on day two, but, when Jesus tells them *he* is the bread, they turn away, grumbling. That was not what they wanted.

John 6 invites us to go deeper into some of the most challenging aspects of our discipleship. It poses some testing questions. What are you looking for from Jesus? Will you offer him what you have? Will you let him feed you? What sort of bread do you crave? Have you recognised that Jesus is the bread from heaven? Finally, like Peter, have you arrived at the place where you can say to Jesus that you have nowhere else to go and that he alone has the words of life?

Over the next ten days, we will travel through this story verse by verse and plumb the depths of its beauty and challenge. The impact of Jesus is difficult as well as attractive and we need to own up to our own mixed responses. Sometimes we are the ones ready to offer the little we have to Jesus; sometimes we are those who turn away, complaining that his teaching is too difficult.

At the end of the story, Peter is able to throw himself on Jesus, not because he has got it all worked out, but because he has seen in Jesus, despite the difficulties, the way to life: 'Lord, to whom can we go?' (v. 68) is what he actually cries out. It's not exactly a profession of faith but an honest assessment that Jesus is the only way, the living bread. I hope we, too, may make the same discovery.

Stephen Cottrell

Where are we to get bread?

After this Jesus went to the other side of the Sea of Galilee... A large crowd kept following him, because they saw the signs that he was doing for the sick. Jesus went up the mountain and sat down there with his disciples... When he looked up and saw a large crowd coming towards him, Jesus said to Philip, 'Where are we to buy bread for these people to eat?' He said this to test him, for he himself knew what he was going to do. Philip answered him, 'Six months' wages would not buy enough bread for each of them to get a little.'

The scene is set for one of Jesus' greatest and most famous miracles, although please note that John calls them 'signs'. He wants us to see what they point to.

Large crowds are following Jesus wherever he goes. They have seen the signs he has performed and are eager to see more.

Jesus goes up a mountain with his disciples. The crowds persist. It is lunchtime; they are hungry. So Jesus says to Philip, 'Where are we to buy bread for these people to eat?' (v. 5). Philip answers, reasonably enough, that 'Six months' wages would not buy enough bread for each of them to get a little' (v. 7).

Let us weigh these few details carefully. First, the mountain is significant. In the Bible, mountains are where you encounter God, so John is preparing us for such an encounter. Second, Jesus' ministry is clearly having a huge impact. The crowd, as we find out later, is vast. Third, Jesus does not just want to teach the crowd, he wants to feed them.

As this chapter develops, we learn about how God wants to minister to all our needs and to the whole person. The crowds who get bread one day will be offered Jesus' very self the next. This offer will be rejected, but, for the time being, we sit at the beginning of the story and ponder the apparent impossibility of the challenge and how it might have felt to Philip. How can such a crowd be fed?

Prayer

Generous God, teach us to look on the impossibilities of the world with the eyes of faith.

STEPHEN COTTRELL

Transforming what we offer

One of his disciples, Andrew, Simon Peter's brother, said to him, 'There is a boy here who has five barley loaves and two fish. But what are they among so many people?' Jesus said, 'Make the people sit down.' Now there was a great deal of grass in the place; so they sat down, about five thousand in all. Then Jesus took the loaves, and when he had given thanks, he distributed them to those who were seated; so also the fish, as much as they wanted.

Reading this story, it is not actually clear whether the small boy contributes his lunch willingly or Andrew requisitions it. I like to think that it is freely given and that Jesus' miracle in some sense proceeds from one person's willingness to offer what they have. Either way, what happens next is astonishing. Even now they have the loaves and fishes, the disciples are as pessimistic as ever: 'But what are they among so many people?' (v. 9), they say, with understandable resignation. The situation does indeed seem hopeless.

This, though, is the God for whom nothing is impossible. This is the God who comes to feed his people. So Jesus sits the crowds down. He takes the bread. He gives thanks. He breaks it. He shares it. This language of taking and blessing and breaking and sharing is the same language the Church now uses in the Eucharist. For, just as Jesus fed the crowds then, he feeds us today.

So here is a question: are we prepared to offer what we have to God or do we think our offering is too small or too insignificant? Do we think the challenges we face are impossible for God? There certainly are challenges in our world: hungry people, terrible injustice, aching chasms between rich and poor. In this story, not only is everyone fed, they have as much as they want, with food left over. It is a picture of God's extravagant and abundant provision. We must not limit this vision. Rather, we need to look again at our own resources, however meagre they may seem, and see what we could hand over for transformation.

Prayer

Abundant God, may the transforming presence of your grace multiply the gifts I offer in service to your world.

STEPHEN COTTRELL

Let nothing be lost

When they were satisfied, he told his disciples, 'Gather up the fragments left over, so that nothing may be lost.' So they gathered them up, and from the fragments of the five barley loaves, left by those who had eaten, they filled twelve baskets.

Before we move on to the rest of this chapter, let us pause and consider these mysterious verses. Jesus instructs his disciples to 'gather up the fragments'. What does this mean and why should it be so important?

Is it an early example of the Countryside Code, Jesus wanting to ensure that there is no litter left from the picnic? Is it to emphasise the enormous plenty that has been miraculously provided? Not only has everyone been fed but also there are twelve baskets of leftovers.

Both these explanations have important things to say to us, but is there something else as well? Is it that nothing is ever wasted for God?

This is the God who counts every hair on your head, the one who sees the smallest sparrow fall (Matthew 10:30). This is the God who, in Christ, takes and honours and multiplies the loaves and fishes that the small boy gives him; he also gathers up every crumb of every banquet.

In the same way, he will not scorn or spurn our offering, however small it is. He will gather up all the fragments of our lives, all the things that we thought were lost or neglected or useless. He is the good shepherd. He knows his sheep; he cares for them; he searches for those that are lost (John 10).

He therefore searches for us and cares for the scattered fragments of our lives. He wants to sit us down and, as we are about to find out, he wants to feed us with himself, if we will let him. For he is the one who tells us that there is rejoicing in heaven over one sinner who repents in the same way that a woman rejoices when she finds a coin that was lost (Luke 15:8–9). So, will we let ourselves be found?

Prayer

Searching God, please look for me. Gather up the fragments of my life and make me whole.

STEPHEN COTTRELL

Don't just do something, sit there

When the people saw the sign that he had done, they began to say, 'This is indeed the prophet who is to come into the world.' When Jesus realised that they were about to come and take him by force to make him king, he withdrew again to the mountain by himself.

The people may not have realised that Jesus is the Messiah, God's word made flesh, but, because of this sign, they did realise he was a great prophet. Amazed by the multiplication of the loaves, they now want to make him king. They project on him all their varied hopes and expectations that God will raise up a king, like David, who will demonstrate, by signs of power, that God has come to liberate his people.

Of course, they are half wrong and half right. Jesus *is* king, but not the sort of king they expect. Nor has his hour yet come. So, Jesus withdraws.

Again, we find ourselves pausing in the narrative, only, this time, the pause is an essential part of the story. It is easy to overlook the fact that Jesus often withdraws to be by himself. He is not simply trying to escape the crowd. Jesus actively seeks a place of contemplation and reflection. He needs time to be with God in order to replenish the reserves of his own obedient service to the Father's will. Eventually he will say, 'Whoever has seen me has seen the Father' (14:9), but Jesus does not arrive at this conclusion all at once. His self-understanding of his vocation to be the Messiah who suffers, and who conquers through obedient, suffering love, is something that grows within him.

This is not easy to understand. Jesus is not God in the disguise of a human being (and therefore able to know all these things clearly and in advance), but God fleshed out within the constraints of our humanity—fully God and, at the same time, fully human. Therefore, his vocation, like ours, develops. We, too, need space for contemplation to discover our vocation and renew our obedience to Christ. We cannot flourish without the pause.

Prayer
Patient God, teach me to watch and wait. Teach me to see and hear.

STEPHEN COTTRELL

Do not be afraid

When evening came, his disciples went down to the lake, got into a boat, and started across the lake to Capernaum. It was now dark, and Jesus had not yet come to them. The lake became rough because a strong wind was blowing. When they had rowed about three or four miles, they saw Jesus walking on the lake and coming near the boat, and they were terrified. But he said to them, 'It is I; do not be afraid.' Then they wanted to take him into the boat, and immediately the boat reached the land towards which they were going.

The disciples have been very busy. They have got hold of a boat and are out on the lake. It is dark. They had hoped Jesus would return, but he had not and they did not wait for him. Instead, they set off for Capernaum. We do not know why; maybe they did not know themselves. In challenging situations sometimes it is a comfort just to do something—it does not really matter what.

They are fishermen, so they put out to sea, but a fierce wind rages. They row and row, but they do not get anywhere. Perhaps stopping and resetting the compass, or at least testing the direction of the wind, might have served them better, but it is too late to do that now. Trapped in the darkness of the night, they fear the stormy waters may engulf them.

Then, in one of those beautifully numinous moments that sparkle throughout the gospel, Jesus appears to them—a still presence in the eye of the storm, walking on the waters. He shows his dominion over the waters, just as God had done in the creation itself. At first they are terrified, but Jesus says, 'It is I; do not be afraid' (v. 20). He identifies himself as 'I am', the mysterious name for God that Moses was to say when asked who sent him (Exodus 3:14). Like Moses delivering God's people from slavery through the waters of the Red Sea, Jesus delivers his disciples safely to the shore.

Will he not calm our fears and guide our feet?

Prayer

Steadfast God, walk to me across the chaos and through the storm, bringing me safely home.

STEPHEN COTTRELL

JOHN 6:22–27 (NRSV, ABRIDGED)

The food that endures

The next day the crowd that had stayed on the other side of the lake saw that there had been only one boat there. They also saw that Jesus had not got into the boat with his disciples, but that his disciples had gone away alone… So… they themselves got into the boats and went to Capernaum looking for Jesus. When they found him on the other side of the lake, they said to him, 'Rabbi, when did you come here?' Jesus answered them, 'Very truly, I tell you, you are looking for me, not because you saw signs, but because you ate your fill of the loaves. Do not work for the food that perishes, but for the food that endures for eternal life, which the Son of Man will give you.'

It is the morning after the night before. Jesus and the disciples are on one side of the lake, the crowds on the other. They go in search of him and, when they find him, noting that he had not left in the boat with the disciples and that no other boat had been used, they ask him how he got there. Jesus refuses to be drawn. He knows why they have pursued him. There was a free lunch yesterday—there may be another one on offer today!

Sadly, this is very typical of how we sometimes respond to God. Dazzled and beguiled by the signs and wonders we sometimes witness, we hold on to them as if they are an end in themselves, rather than recognising them as signposts to the ultimate healing and provision that can only come direct from God. Most of the rest of this chapter is a long and hugely important address by Jesus on learning to search for the right food—not bread that perishes, like the perishable stuff in a perishable world, but something that endures for eternal life.

This world, and all that is in it, will come to an end, but there is another food that endures for eternity. Jesus has come to give it to us.

Prayer

Generous God, move us from the signposts of your glory to the reality of your grace.

STEPHEN COTTRELL

I am the bread

They said to him, 'What must we do to perform the works of God?' Jesus answered them, 'This is the work of God, that you believe in him whom he has sent.' So they said to him, 'What sign are you going to give us, so that we may see it and believe you?... Our ancestors ate the manna in the wilderness...' Jesus said to them, 'Very truly, I tell you, it was not Moses who gave you the bread from heaven, but it is my Father who gives you the true bread from heaven. For the bread of God is that which comes down from heaven and gives life to the world.' They said to him, 'Sir, give us this bread always.' Jesus said to them, 'I am the bread of life. Whoever comes to me will never be hungry, and whoever believes in me will never be thirsty.'

The discussion continues. Still hung up on signs and wonders, the people question Jesus, asking what sign he will give them. Their ancestors had been given manna in the desert, so what will Jesus give? They seem to have forgotten about yesterday's lunch, but Jesus persists: 'it was not Moses who gave you the bread from heaven, but it is my Father who gives you the true bread from heaven. For the bread of God is that which comes down from heaven and gives life to the world' (v. 32). In reply, they ask to be given this wonderful bread. 'I am the bread of life,' says Jesus (v. 35).

This astonishing announcement is the heart of the chapter. Everything else flows from it and to it. As noted, the words 'I am', which Jesus uses throughout John's Gospel, are themselves an indication of Jesus taking to himself the sacred name revealed to Moses, but now he says, 'I am the bread of life. Whoever comes to me will never be hungry, and whoever believes in me will never be thirsty' (v. 35). It is not yesterday's loaves, but Jesus himself who is the bread the world needs.

Prayer

Welcoming God, help me to come to Jesus and never be hungry;
help me believe in him and never thirst.

STEPHEN COTTRELL

This is my body, broken for you

The Jews began to complain about him... saying, 'Is not this Jesus, the son of Joseph...? How can he now say, "I have come down from heaven"?' Jesus answered them, 'Do not complain among yourselves. No one can come to me unless drawn by the Father who sent me; and I will raise that person up on the last day... Very truly, I tell you, whoever believes has eternal life. I am the bread of life. Your ancestors ate the manna in the wilderness, and they died. This is the bread that comes down from heaven, so that one may eat of it and not die... Whoever eats of this bread will live for ever; and the bread that I will give for the life of the world is my flesh.'

It is impossible for us to read these amazing words today without thinking of the Eucharist. In John's Gospel there is no account of the Last Supper, because of John's different chronology for the whole passion narrative, but, in this chapter, he is consciously pointing us towards the central truths of the Christian faith that are commemorated and renewed whenever Holy Communion is celebrated and shared.

The people may complain that this is 'only Joseph's son', but that is the whole point. God has come to us in the likeness of our own frail flesh. God has come down from heaven in order to raise us up. Also, Jesus is the true bread. Not bread like the miraculous loaves that the people shared, not bread like the manna eaten in the wilderness, but the bread that has come down from heaven in Jesus so that those who partake of him will live forever.

The broken bread and poured out wine of his body and blood are given for the life of the world. If we eat this bread—which has the double meaning of 'if we believe in Jesus and make our home in him' and 'if we are faithful to breaking bread and sharing wine in remembrance of him'—then we have a share in eternal life.

Prayer

Feed us with the bread of eternal life, which is Jesus our Saviour, and keep us faithful to him.

STEPHEN COTTRELL

The gift of life

The Jews then disputed among themselves, saying, 'How can this man give us his flesh to eat?' So Jesus said to them, 'Very truly, I tell you, unless you eat the flesh of the Son of Man and drink his blood, you have no life in you. Those who eat my flesh and drink my blood have eternal life, and I will raise them up on the last day; for my flesh is true food and my blood is true drink... This is the bread that came down from heaven, not like that which your ancestors ate, and they died. But the one who eats this bread will live for ever.'

'How can this man give us his flesh to eat?' (v. 52). Good question.

Jesus' whole life and ministry, passion, death and resurrection are food for the human spirit. Jesus is the mediator of the gift of life God the Father wants to give to the world—and we need to receive the gift of his life laid down. 'It does not earn us eternal life,' said William Temple, that great Archbishop of Canterbury, 'it is eternal life'.

Jesus specifically speaks of the need to 'eat my flesh and drink my blood' (v. 54). This is shocking and graphic language, especially for Jews who were specifically forbidden to drink blood (Deuteronomy 12:23), but here it means that we must receive the life given through his death.

This again points us to that perpetual remembrance of Christ's passion, the Eucharist. Here in bread and wine we receive the body and blood of Jesus. Next time you receive Holy Communion, remember, you are not feeding on a corpse, nor passively reimagining what Jesus did in the past, but partaking in the living reality of communion with the risen Jesus. The sacrament we receive is an end in itself. It is communion with God, but also a means to an end. It points beyond itself to the reality it communicates, which is the eternal abiding with God that Jesus makes possible. The manna eaten in the desert lasted but a moment; those who eat this bread live for ever.

Prayer

Give us this bread always!

STEPHEN COTTRELL

Where else can we go?

When many of his disciples heard it, they said, 'This teaching is difficult; who can accept it?' But Jesus, being aware that his disciples were complaining about it, said to them, 'Does this offend you? Then what if you were to see the Son of Man ascending to where he was before? It is the spirit that gives life; the flesh is useless. The words that I have spoken to you are spirit and life.'… Because of this many of his disciples turned back and no longer went about with him. So Jesus asked the twelve, 'Do you also wish to go away?' Simon Peter answered him, 'Lord, to whom can we go? You have the words of eternal life. We have come to believe and know that you are the Holy One of God.'

It is a heart-rending paradox of the gospel that such a beautiful and triumphant chapter ends with such disappointment. Jesus' words, which are spirit and life, fall on deaf ears. The very public declaration of his mission—he is the living bread come down from heaven—is also bewildering and frightening. As a consequence, many leave him. 'This teaching is difficult', say the disciples; 'who can accept it?' and they complain among themselves.

The crowds depart and many of the wider band of Jesus' followers slip away.

Jesus is left alone with the Twelve. He turns to them and says, 'Do you also wish to go away?' (v. 67). If we are honest, I suppose we must conclude that they probably did, just as we often find Jesus' teaching difficult and his demands horribly challenging. Peter, however, speaks for all of us, too, when he replies, 'Lord, to whom can we go?' (v. 68), which I understand to mean, 'Lord, we would love to go somewhere else, but in you we have caught a glimpse of God's purposes and God's love, so there is no turning back. You, and you alone have the words of eternal life.'

Prayer

Generous God, we believe that Jesus alone has the words of eternal life and that his life laid down is food and drink for a needy world. Feed us with this living bread and enable us always to abide in him.

STEPHEN COTTRELL

My favourite scriptures

As a young Christian, I have to confess, I never knew that the Bible was actually meant to be read! I can recall friends discussing things such as 'Romans' or 'Ephesians' with enthusiasm, but I had not got a clue what they were talking about. When I received a Bible at 17 years of age from my mother, I noticed that there were some portions of scripture set out on the inside cover and, because I had no idea how biblical references were presented, I came to the conclusion that these must be general warnings about adultery and reckless behaviour, rather than Bible quotes! I thought it a little harsh, to put it mildly…

The series of notes we are about to embark on is designed to show what I now know about how the Bible might be used properly, how wonderful it is and how it speaks to us personally and to a huge array of real-life situations. If the scriptures are God's word, then we should expect God to speak to us directly through them, but also we should expect to find there guidance about the way Christians are called to be disciples. That word 'disciple' is a critical one in our vocabulary because it includes not only the issues of daily life, such as how we learn to pray, but also issues of national and international significance, such as justice and poverty.

In writing these notes, I have tried to say something about my own journey in relation to God and about those themes that have been transformational for my thinking. At the same time, I hope there are wider resonances, too, and these may help you begin to find that your own walk with God is both enriched and informed as you read what I have to share over the next couple of weeks. In an age when too many either look for wisdom in strange places, such as horoscopes and tarot, or, conversely, have no recourse to any received wisdom, the Bible retains its unique capacity to speak afresh and console, challenge and open new avenues for individuals and churches alike. I pray that this series will move you on to a deeper engagement with it and to the One who inspired its writing.

Andy John

A moment of grace

And we know that in all things God works for the good of those who love him, who have been called according to his purpose.

Confession time: I am not overly acquainted with vacuum cleaners. I think I know how they work—at least in theory—but I would be bending the truth if I stated that our relationship went much further. That is why it is so extraordinary that one of my deepest encounters with God was when I was actually using one!

Picture the scene: someone had seriously put my nose out of joint and I was using the vacuum cleaner as my weapon of release as I bent God's ear about the injustice I had suffered. The complaint was typically rambling, self-pitying and selfish. Then God asked 'What is more important, your satisfaction or the blessings that this situation will bring to many people?' I felt reduced to dust, bringing a new sense to the words 'I spoke of things I did not understand' (Job 42:3).

You might think that story is a little frivolous, especially when we consider some of the big issues of today, such as poverty, refugees, terrorism and war, but I think it indicates God's purposes—even when they are missed or obstructed by human beings—are always to redeem and to renew. The God of our Lord Jesus Christ is the God of resurrection and new life, in which the curse of sin is turned upside down so that new instances of grace and growth are made possible. When we are brought to this realisation, it offers us the chance to align our attitudes and lives with God's good purposes. For me, this was a turning point in my relationship with God. Take the opportunity now to ask, 'How is God working for good in my life—and is there space enough to listen, hear and respond?'

Prayer

Gracious God, you open the closed minds of men and women with the light of your love. Help us to let that searching love penetrate ever deeper into each of us so that new and holy acts of love might grow in us. For Christ's sake. Amen

ANDY JOHN

Love unyielding

"'My son,' the father said, "you are always with me, and everything I have is yours. But we had to celebrate and be glad, because this brother of yours was dead and is alive again; he was lost and is found.'"

Countless preachers and commentators have wrestled with this story. Is it about the love of the father who waits patiently for his younger son until he returns? Is it about the hard pride of the older son who offers loyalty although he misunderstands true love? Is it about the profligate who blows it all and yet discovers there is always a way back, even from the abyss?

I want to concentrate on how the story ends for both sons because, at this point, we see most clearly the unyielding love of God. For the younger son, the return is full of fear and perhaps self-interested hopes of restoration. Our motives in repentance are perhaps never as clear-cut as we might like to admit, but this is, nonetheless, met with abundant grace (vv. 22–24). Why? Because the nature of God requires it. He is full of grace and love for his wayward and self-absorbed world. His love is undiminished by sin, even when his heart breaks and wrath is kindled.

The elder son's story shows a life of deep loyalty, in contrast to that of his brother, but the discovery of his brother's return 'blows the lid off' this persona. In verses 31–32 the dialogue turns from this son's anger to the father's entreating and, at the end, the father is still pleading with his son to be reconciled with his long-lost brother. The point in both encounters is the way the father's extraordinary love reaches out equally to his two sons without bending or breaking.

Where does this story find you today? Do you find yourself closer to one of the sons and how might God's unyielding love reach out to you today?

Prayer

Lord Jesus, you open the character of the Father's love in ways that thrill and disturb us. May your Holy Spirit's persistence contain grace enough to win us to a new faith and obedience for the Father's glory. Amen

ANDY JOHN

Rich poverty

Now when Jesus saw the crowds, he went up on a mountainside and sat down. His disciples came to him, and he began to teach them. He said: 'Blessed are the poor in spirit, for theirs is the kingdom of heaven.'

The Beatitudes rank among the most famous parts of the scriptures, although they are probably among the most misunderstood, too. If we read them carefully, it becomes clear that they have little to do with vague idealism and, instead, present a radical agenda involving the transformation of attitudes and actions. Both Matthew and Luke contain accounts of these sayings and, although they vary slightly in the two Gospels, they are given to us as central to the emerging ministry of Jesus.

So Jesus sees the crowd of followers, like Moses the great leader in the Old Testament, and he begins to teach his disciples. The first saying is about being poor. It would be monstrous if we thought poverty was being commended in this verse. Poverty is not commended here, nor, I believe, at any point in scripture.

So, what is the poverty commended here? It would be better to speak of it in relation to attitudes reflecting modesty in possessing and generosity in giving. It is the formation of an inner life in view of God's boundless mercy and love and our own weakness and sin. The two combine to produce this radically different assessment of ourselves— not so self-absorbed that we sit at the centre without regard for others, with God's only role being that of fulfilling our desires and aspirations. Neither does it mean being crushed by a vision of God and ourselves in which there is no value to life and no escape from sin. I know how much I need the kind of poverty that keeps me from self-serving acts, yet holds the hope of a better and alternative vision of life always before me. Without it there is no kingdom.

Prayer

Lord Jesus, true teacher and giver of wisdom, may I perceive what this verse could mean for me today and be inspired to challenge complacent attitudes and let your values become my own. Amen

ANDY JOHN

Ancient paths

This is what the Lord says: 'Stand at the crossroads and look; ask for the ancient paths, ask where the good way is, and walk in it, and you will find rest for your souls.'

I have long been intrigued by the film *Castaway*, starring Tom Hanks. It tells the story of one man who has crash-landed on a desert island and faces the challenge of survival. At the end, Hanks, having lost almost all that was dear to him prior to the plane crash, stands at a crossroads, viewing the dilemmas this break with his previous life creates. Is this a sad moment for him, surveying what he has lost, or does it mark a new start—a life beginning to unfold with new and fresh opportunities?

In today's passage, the prophet Jeremiah calls God's people to stand at the crossroads and choose. What lie before them are the 'ancient paths' and the 'good ways', representing the ways of God, tried and tested, which bring 'rest for the soul'. What makes the picture so compelling is that the responsibility lies with the hearer.

When we induct a new minister in Bangor diocese, the liturgy uses the phrase 'which faith the church is called upon to preach afresh in every generation'. It is an evocative picture because it draws on the idea of the ancient path, what is known to be true and good, but infuses it with new urgency and contemporary appeal, that faith must be made new in each generation. I find this idea challenging because it means I cannot rely on yesterday's experience of God for any lack in my faith today. The ways of God, firm and true, must be appropriated today; ancient faith must live in the now if I am to follow Christ closely.

How does this picture speak to you, I wonder? In the daily challenges of your life, where might you find ancient paths leading to new faith and ways of following Christ?

Prayer

Ancient of Days, your ways are good and true and bring rest for the soul. In the everyday matters, help me to see the choices before me with the eyes of faith and help me to choose what is good and true. In Jesus' name.
Amen

ANDY JOHN

Our God who sees

You have searched me, Lord, and you know me. You know when I sit and when I rise; you perceive my thoughts from afar. You discern my going out and my lying down; you are familiar with all my ways.

This is a psalm whose every verse I would love to include in this commentary. Why? Because it is the reflection of a believer who knows that God is to be found everywhere and is all-wise and all-caring.

Many years ago, I came across the idea of 'God walks'—walking outside, perhaps in the hills or somewhere quiet, where the context allows deep thinking, prayer and reflection. I have wondered if this psalm was written in such a way.

The all-encompassing, all-knowing God is our creator and redeemer, whose knowledge of us is as intimate as he is infinite. I sometimes marvel at how people conceive of God. Very often, though, his greatness is cast in terms that are positively terrifying. Meeting such a God would not seem a very pleasant prospect, but the reflections in this beautiful psalm lead us to a different view—the strength and greatness of God is attractive, if elusive.

Many people have found C.S. Lewis's depiction of the Narnian Christ-figure Aslan, as a lion who is 'not tame', to be powerful and real. The God presented to us here is, likewise, beyond us, incapable of being boxed in, even as we discover something of his extraordinary care and goodness.

I wonder if the ground of our thinking needs to shift here? This great God has complete knowledge of us, which should actually invite wonder and praise rather than morbid dread. I wonder, too, if periods of quiet and reflection might allow this kind of psalm to rise afresh in our prayer and thinking. May it be so for you today.

Prayer

God of heaven and earth, you hold all things in your hands and yet you know each one of us. Teach us to recognise in your infinite power your infinite care and to love you with all our energy and strength. Amen

ANDY JOHN

The back of God

> Then the Lord said, 'There is a place near me where you may stand on a rock. When my glory passes by, I will put you in a cleft in the rock and cover you with my hand until I have passed by. Then I will remove my hand and you will see my back; but my face must not be seen.'

When Moses asked God to be present with the people of Israel on their journey, he had more than his own credibility as leader in mind. Our verses today are a wonderful example of how each of us needs the sort of divine encounter that builds faith and trust, yet they also show the tender mercy and gentle, gracious care of God. Such themes are not always obvious in the Old Testament, but here we see them strongly. God places Moses in a cleft in the rock and covers him with a protecting hand so that Moses is not overwhelmed by the encounter. We read, too, that Moses shall see only the 'back of God'.

Two things strike me here. First, God only discloses just enough of himself as is necessary for a given time. I have found myself sometimes, perhaps often, wondering why I cannot see the way ahead as clearly as I would like. In fact, it is a mercy that God does not show us everything, but the right amount to keep us trusting and walking in faith.

Second, many people have found the idea of seeing the 'back of God' suggestive. Sometimes the presence and action of God are more obvious to us sometime later, after an issue has been resolved and when we have reflected on the situation. Then we have seen how God was present and active. We see, figuratively, the 'back' of God, the evidence of his work.

Does this resonate with you today and how might these verses help you to walk forward with new faith and trust?

Prayer
Gracious and caring God, show me enough of yourself to keep me close and give me new eyes to see how and where you are at work in my life and in others around me, too. For Christ's sake. Amen

ANDY JOHN

2 Chronicles 20:12 (NIV)

Eyes on God

'Our God, will you not judge them? For we have no power to face this vast army that is attacking us. We do not know what to do, but our eyes are on you.'

I suspect many are familiar with what are termed 'arrow prayers'—when we send our words heavenwards, perhaps in an emergency or because we do not know what else to do. Although there is a great deal more to prayer, there is nothing wrong with such an approach and bringing God to the fore in our lives is always a good thing.

Today's passage has a particular and dramatic context. At the time, Jehoshaphat is the king of Judah and facing a serious threat from surrounding armies. In the face of this threat, he assembles many people and leads them in a sort of arrow prayer (vv. 6–12). First of all, it is an appeal to God's own character and actions (vv. 6–9). This is a familiar pattern in the Bible and underlines the basis of all prayer, which is that God always hears us and is always able to respond. Prayer is not therefore simply an expression of human need but also an appeal to one who can surely answer. The prayer is also open and 'waiting' (v. 12), in the sense that the king does not know what the outcome might be but trusts nonetheless.

This last point is especially important. There have been times when I have prayed without knowing what the best outcome in a situation might be. Jehoshaphat shows us that leaving the outcome to God is not an abdication of faith but actually a trusting and faithful prayer. It places us in that area of dependence where we acknowledge it is God's solution that is needed.

What situations do you face today that are like this? 'Our eyes are on you' might be the very prayer you need and leaving God to respond may be a liberating and comforting decision.

Prayer

Lord, you know all things and you know what is both needed in my life and best for my life. Teach me to fix my eyes on you in trust and faith. Through the grace of Jesus Christ. Amen

Andy John

Grace and truth

For the law was given through Moses; grace and truth came through Jesus Christ.

The whole of chapter 1 of John's Gospel is unlike anything else in the Bible. We call these first verses the 'prologue' because they introduce the good news about Jesus and tell us how to read and understand everything that follows. The title used for the last passage read at the traditional service of the Nine Lessons and Carols at Christmas usually goes like this: 'St John unfolds the great mystery of the incarnation'. It means that John's purpose is to show how God has come to us in Jesus.

This idea is present in our passage today but is conveyed via a contrast: Moses brought the Law from God, but grace and truth came from Jesus. The point about this contrast is that it moves us from knowing what is right and good (the Law) to being able to live for God in a new way. Grace is God's great enabling characteristic and one of the dominant ideas in the New Testament. It is all about how God deals with his creation as a loving Saviour.

In the life, death and resurrection of Jesus, this idea is given special force because those events are the means by which people are forgiven and restored. Somehow, in a wonderful exchange, all that is from God becomes ours in Jesus when we believe and respond to him. The early Christians used the dramatic picture of baptism to describe this: plunging beneath the waters to symbolise dying to the old way of life apart from God and rising up to a new life of service and holiness.

The God who won us, despite ourselves and without our assistance, continues his grace towards us through his Spirit so that we are always being urged and enabled to live faithful Christian lives. Today, rejoice that God is full of grace, which is turned towards you, and let it win you afresh.

Prayer

God of grace, you sent Jesus to win and save us. May your grace win us afresh today and consume all that is weak and wrong in us. May our lives be ever shaped by your grace and truth. In Jesus' name. Amen

ANDY JOHN

New every morning

Because of the Lord's great love we are not consumed, for his compassions never fail. They are new every morning; great is your faithfulness.

As a young Christian, I regularly sang a chorus based on these words and I found that it spoke deeply to me about God's steadfast love, although I had little idea where the words came from in the Bible. Any reading of the book of Lamentations will show you that it is well named, which makes these two verses stand out even more strongly. Against the background of sorrows they jump out from the pages and offer much-needed encouragement. Although throughout the Bible there are many verses similar to these, it is the use of the word 'compassions' that sets these particular verses apart.

What does the author mean by 'compassions'? It is a word of tender and patient regard. When we say that God is compassionate, we are saying something about how God responds and acts towards human beings. Here the word is in the plural, so that what is in view are God's many acts of tender regard, which is why I find this passage so compelling. It tells me that God is consistently beholding my weaknesses with neither disdain nor cold indifference, still less with anger or rejection, but with kindness and care. This is true for all people. God has compassion for those whose situations are desperate and who cry out to him, for those who are lost or unloved, those in pain or who suffer in any other way.

It can be hard to recognise God's compassions at times because situations can overwhelm us. We may feel trapped and alone in our desperation, but this is when we need to hear these words anew. Like a light piercing the gloom, they can lift us and remind us that we are not abandoned but, rather, held very securely in the compassionate and tender love of God.

Prayer

Lord God, your compassions never fail and are new every morning. May I discover this today for myself and for those around me who need your comfort and help. In Jesus' name. Amen

ANDY JOHN

ECCLESIASTES 3:1–2 (NIV)

A time and season for everything

There is a time for everything, and a season for every activity under the heavens: a time to be born and a time to die, a time to plant and a time to uproot.

Ecclesiastes might not be the most widely read book in the Old Testament, but there are few who would not know these extraordinary words from the 'Teacher', who narrates it: 'There is a time for everything, and a season for every activity under the heavens' (v. 1). In what some consider to be a book that is overly anxious, to the point of bordering on the manically depressed, these words of wise restraint and acceptance show the level of careful and profound reflection that has taken place in the soul of the writer. They invite a kind of engagement that takes us way beyond the places of superficiality that characterise so much 'quick fix' commentary today. In their stead we are invited to think on how life has its boundaries, its balances, its contours and, of course, with it, a context in which to practise faithful Christian living.

So how does this passage help us? First, I think it gives us perspective. The reality of fallible and finite human life is the arena in which we live. Even as I write these words, I think of two people I know who have suffered terrible bereavements. Words cannot comfort them yet, but perhaps in time the understanding that we are all frail can help to guard against any feelings of injustice and a brooding sense that life has 'betrayed' us. Second, they can help us focus on what is sure and certain. In the Old Testament this certainty might have centred on the greatness of God; in the New Testament it is shown to rest on the promises of Jesus, whose presence with us is assured and unwavering. When we feel the waters threatening to overwhelm us, this text is a gentle pointing to what cannot die and will not fail.

Prayer

Father in heaven, you have ordered life with its joys and sadnesses. Give us gifts of wisdom and a confident trust that, whatever life may bring, your eternal strength will always uphold us. In Jesus' name. Amen

ANDY JOHN

Making earthquakes

After the Sabbath, at dawn on the first day of the week, Mary Magdalene and the other Mary went to look at the tomb. There was a violent earthquake, for an angel of the Lord came down from heaven and, going to the tomb, rolled back the stone and sat on it.

We are fortunate in the UK in that we rarely suffer earthquakes. In 2013, there was one in North Wales that shook my house in Bangor and then sounded like a huge lorry moving off into the distance, grumbling as it went. I cannot imagine how terrifying it must be to experience something more serious and longer-lasting than the ten seconds of shudder we endured. It is somewhat alarming, then, to read how an angel appears to have shifted the continental plates and then moved an admittedly smaller, but nonetheless extremely heavy, rock as part of the announcement of the resurrection of Jesus.

We might well ask what is going on in Matthew's account of this seminal event for the whole world. It is, of course, all about drama. Not cheap conjuring tricks but, rather, this is an event that is meant to be felt as much as any other physical event.

Look at the words again. The angel makes a mockery of death by rolling away the stone and sitting on it. An earthquake disrupts the daily course of life and shows that God's sovereign power is being wielded. We are meant to see the significance of the occasion by the events that accompany them. This is no ordinary happening. It changes everything because the ultimate certainty in the universe—death itself—is struck down by the power of resurrection life.

As I read this episode, it has fresh power to inspire and challenge because the resurrection of Jesus should cause earthquakes—in our lives and communities, nation and world. I wonder if I could be a part of a different drama—one in which that resurrection life is seen in me.

Prayer

Lord Jesus, risen and ascended king, may your power be at work in me today and shown in weakness and strength, all for the glory of your name.

ANDY JOHN

Great joy for all the people

But the angel said to them, 'Do not be afraid. I bring you good news that will cause great joy for all the people. Today in the town of David a Saviour has been born to you; he is the Messiah, the Lord.'

I never tire of hearing those words—in the Christmas season or at any time of the year. The announcement of the Saviour's birth stands alongside that other angelic announcement, 'He is not here; he has risen!' (24:6). Both are seminal and the words bring together ancient hopes and sacred story in an altogether unexpected way because God's deliverance would not come with thunder and lightning, fiery mountain and raging tempest, but quietly, in a small provincial town on the outskirts of civilisation. This great news of great joy is all wrapped up in swaddling bands, but, more importantly, wrapped up in frail humanity. This great news is also given gently, lest the hearers be overwhelmed: 'Do not be afraid' (v. 10). Although this is to allay the fear of the shepherds at what must have been an incredible sight, it has some deeper significance. The coming of God should not bring dread, but deepest joy. These words hold out that hope for us all—'for all the people', the angel said (v. 10).

This message speaks to me not only of God's deep solidarity with his world but also his saving grace. We do not follow a distant deity, far beyond us, but one who has leapt into all the world's pain and misery and grown up among us as one of us. His coming is to make us his own, to bring peace to all people and reach everyone with his saving love.

I wonder how this message touches us afresh today, as it invites our wholehearted response. Whatever we feel about ourselves, whatever good or ills we may have done, God loves us entirely and completely. Does this not demand my all?

Prayer

Lord Jesus, born as a child and one of us, you are the Saviour come to save all people. May your love reach me and many others today so that we may be transformed by that love into the people you created us to be. Amen

ANDY JOHN

Winds and waves

[Jesus] got up, rebuked the wind and said to the waves, 'Quiet!
Be still!' Then the wind died down and it was completely calm. He
said to his disciples, 'Why are you so afraid? Do you still have no
faith?' They were terrified and asked each other, 'Who is this?
Even the wind and the waves obey him!'

Some of the Gospel stories seem fantastic and, while I have no difficulty
in believing them, I sometimes wonder why some seem more 'miraculous' than others. It would be absurd to read these words other than as
Mark intends, namely as a miracle that brings about the saving of lives
and new faith. I think it must speak to us, too, in our own moments of
deep crisis when we feel tossed about, at sea with no one to help us.

Look at the words again—how Jesus commands the wind and
waves. They are stilled and he challenges the disciples' lack of belief.
They are 'moved' to a new kind of faith. Similarly, into the chaos of our
lives Jesus speaks a word that calms fears and allows all that is troubled
to be overcome. It is an act of gracious and powerful love that needs no
other response than faith and acceptance.

The astonishment of the disciples marks real progress; they are different as a consequence of this encounter. There is a way of viewing
discipleship that 'goes soft' on this second dimension. We find Christ
helping us, but we do not allow this experience to result in renewed
faith and obedience. This may be because we do not yet have 'eyes to
see' or because we do not reflect on what this encounter means.
Alternatively, it may be because we do not want to move on, being too
comfortable where we are.

Are there seas of chaos threatening you? Winds and waves of
despair? Jesus calls you to let him calm what is troubled and allow new
faith to emerge and grow.

Prayer

Lord Jesus, speak your word of calm and let that word silence my chaos.
Give me new understanding of the way your grace can overcome in me and
in others all that prevents us from loving and following you. For your sake.
Amen

ANDY JOHN

Love without limit

And I pray that you, being rooted and established in love, may have power, together with all the Lord's holy people, to grasp how wide and long and high and deep is the love of Christ, and to know this love that surpasses knowledge—that you may be filled to the measure of all the fullness of God.

Can you remember when you first realised that God loved you? I can remember to this very day and the effect it had on me. All that I had believed about Christians and Christianity was blown apart. I realised that there was nothing better, more urgent or more wonderful than making that love known to others.

In our verses today, the writer lifts his description of the love of Christ to new heights in a wonderful prayer for the Ephesian Christians. To pray this prayer is to be immersed in that very love. We cannot pray with this kind of intensity without knowing that love ourselves and knowing it can pass into a kind of desire that others might taste and see for themselves how wide, long, high and deep is this love.

Here we must reflect on the cross and how Jesus gave himself for our sins. In his dying and rising again we see the reality of his love, which continues each day. There is nothing more powerful in the world that can change a person's heart, make friends out of enemies and transform the all but impossible conflicts we see around us. It is this love that the church is called to share and it is this love which has the capacity to make life worth living.

Is this love real to you and, if so, who are those who might come to know it a little better because you have tasted and seen? Pray today for friends, colleagues, family and neighbours that the love of Christ might be known in all its fullness. There is nothing more important than this.

Prayer

O God, may your eternal love reach through and beyond me to many others, so they may know the greatest treasure of all and also the cost of such wonderful blessing. Amen

ANDY JOHN

Songs of praise: 'Dear Lord and Father'

The hymn 'Dear Lord and Father of mankind' is one of the most popular. It came second (to 'How great Thou art') in a BBC *Songs of Praise* poll for Britain's favourite hymn in 2005. This is surely in part because of the wonderful tune to which it is usually sung—'Repton' by Hubert Parry. It might come as a surprise to hear, though, that, in the United States, it usually goes with completely different music. That 'other' tune, unlike Repton, does not repeat the last line of each verse. In my view, it is decent enough, but lacks Repton's lyrical and soothing qualities, which seem to add drama to 'the beauty of Thy peace'.

The words of the hymn are taken from a much longer poem, 'The Brewing of Soma', written in 1872 by American Quaker writer and journalist John Greenleaf Whittier (1807–92). The work as a whole describes the attempts by other religions and some Christians to approach God by methods such as 'music, incense, vigils drear, And trance', which the author dismisses as intoxication. He contrasts these with Quaker ways, of seeking God in silence and selfless action. So, it is ironic that his words have now become part of what can be a mesmerising experience. Whittier also wrote a number of other poems that were set to music as hymns, including 'Immortal love, forever full'.

The tune 'Repton' was written in 1888, but only paired with the hymn in 1924, after the death of the composer, the distinguished professor of music Sir Hubert Parry (1848–1918). Despite this, the words and music seem to combine seamlessly to suggest much more than the sum of their parts. The calming harmonies prompt me to probe and ponder my own life, so I believe that the prayers expressed in the hymn, addressed directly to God—'Reclothe us in our rightful mind', 'Speak through the earthquake, wind, and fire'—relate straight back to my experience and place it in God's care.

All this is very much a personal, emotional response, but I see the blend of words and music as conveying a psychological depth, delving into my motivation and, crucially, spurring me on to seek God. I wonder what effect it has on you.

Rachel Boulding

FAITH **Sunday 8 February** *TRUTH*

MATTHEW 6:9–10, 12–15 (NRSV)

Our loving Father ② 8am

'Pray then in this way: Our Father in heaven, hallowed be your name. Your kingdom come, your will be done, on earth as it is in heaven... And forgive us our debts, as we also have forgiven our debtors. And do not bring us to the time of trial, but rescue us from the evil one. For if you forgive others their trespasses, your heavenly Father will also forgive you; but if you do not forgive others, neither will your Father forgive your trespasses.'

'Dear Lord and Father of mankind, Forgive our foolish ways…' These opening lines are in many ways the most important of the whole hymn—they are the ones that everyone knows and quotes. More than that, they set the tone of an affectionate prayer to God—he is our 'Dear Lord' and the father of us all. We have a connection with him and a relationship of love. Yes, he is always our Lord, but he is a '*Dear* Lord'. He is our father, and a loving one. As Jesus makes clear in giving us the Lord's Prayer, we can talk to him at any time.

By calling him Father in this way, we approach him as his own children, secure in our relationship to him, but still aware of our failings. Perhaps we have failed in a childish way: we might well have behaved self-centredly, like a child who thinks the world should revolve around him or herself. 'Forgive our foolish ways' is a line that speaks to us and probes our deepest sense of ourselves. We know, fundamentally, that we have done wrong. We have been silly in ridiculous ways or stupid in wilful, deliberate wrongdoing.

So, we are presented with a contrast: on one side, the loving, perfect father and, on the other, ourselves—sinful and foolish. These opening lines bring these two together straight away. We know we do not have to stay mired in our guilt, we can turn to our Father and join in this prayer for forgiveness. We have a home to go to with God.

Prayer

Help me to turn to you, dear Lord and Father, whenever I am aware of my sin. Amen

RACHEL BOULDING

JUSTIFIED AND SET STRAIGHT

Worship leading to wholeness

Give unto the Lord the glory due unto his name: bring an offering, and come into his courts. O worship the Lord in the beauty of holiness: fear before him, all the earth. Say among the heathen that the Lord reigneth: the world also shall be established that it shall not be moved: he shall judge the people righteously. Let the heavens rejoice, and let the earth be glad.

'Reclothe us in our rightful mind, In purer lives thy service find, In deeper reverence, praise.' The longing for worship depicted in Psalm 96 links with the rest of the first verse of this hymn, in that both vividly convey the beauty of holiness and the powerful attraction of praising God. Many of us have had the most important experiences of our lives during worship, but they are not things that make sense to everyone. It is easy to misunderstand, for rejoicing in spirituality can topple over into spiritual pride—as Jesus repeatedly warned the devout people of his own time.

The desire to worship is fundamentally a good urge, however. If we neglect it, we miss something of God's creation. Unusually, the hymn weaves together such praise and reverence with healing and the rediscovery of our whole selves. The connections might not be obvious, but there is a sense of our reaching to something beyond ourselves, which takes us out of our 'foolish ways'. The direction leads away from our twisted 'sweating selves', as the poet Gerard Manley Hopkins put it, in his harrowing evocation of night terrors, 'I wake and feel the fell of dark, not day'. Even when we feel devastated like this, we can be drawn towards God's ultimate goodness.

Worship can direct us away from our limitations and towards a truer perspective, which places God at the centre. We can hardly think of God, the creator of the universe, who is also our own dear Lord, without a sense of reverence and this leads on directly to praise. Tracing this process has a certain logic and can set us on the right path—thus leaving our foolish ways behind and turning towards God.

Reflection

'Show me your paths… guide me by your truth' Psalm 25:4 (CEV).

RACHEL BOULDING

Follow the Lord, right now

And Jesus, walking by the sea of Galilee, saw two brethren, Simon called Peter, and Andrew his brother, casting a net into the sea: for they were fishers. And he saith unto them, Follow me, and I will make you fishers of men. And they straightway left their nets, and followed him.

'In simple trust like theirs who heard, Beside the Syrian sea, The gracious calling of the Lord, Let us, like them, without a word, Rise up and follow thee.'

Now, I must confess that I have a perhaps irrational bad reaction to the word 'simple'. It is not just that it can imply 'stupid' in some settings but also, so often, people seem to urge simplicity only after huge complexities or even as part of some nostalgic fantasy. If everything were really a matter of returning to some imagined state of straightforwardness in a traditional society, we would all be able to do this easily (and simply). I like the modern world, though. Technological advances have made my life much easier than that of my grandparents—and probably longer, too, as I have been treated for cancer.

If we are not careful, we can be tempted to think it was not a difficult choice for the disciples—that they *could* just take off with Jesus. But were their lives, in fact, so different in this respect from modern Western ones? The disciples had family responsibilities and had to earn a living, without the safety net of a welfare state. In some ways, it is easier for people now to set off in search of spiritual truths, as many do, when they go travelling the world.

Perhaps I should try to dig deeper and get to what I imagine is the writer's intention here. That is, the sense in which we can all—no matter how entangled our lives are—follow Christ. There are ways in which this could not be simpler. We can turn to Christ, right now, for his is a 'gracious calling'—not a strident demand, but a gentle, generous invitation—that we are free to reject if we please.

Reflection

What excuses will I make today for not immediately following Jesus?

RACHEL BOULDING

MATTHEW 14:22–23 (NRSV)

Join Jesus in the silence

Immediately he made the disciples get into the boat and go on ahead to the other side, while he dismissed the crowds. And after he had dismissed the crowds, he went up the mountain by himself to pray. When evening came, he was there alone.

'O sabbath rest by Galilee, O calm of hills above, where Jesus knelt to share with thee the silence of eternity, interpreted by love!' Verse 3 takes us on to more solid ground. Here is some practical action that we can all join in with—spending some time in prayer. Our prayer time can be the most important minutes of the day, even if they are very few indeed. What else could we be doing that is more important than reminding ourselves we are in the presence of God?

My friend was visiting from Lancashire and we met in London. She was amazed at how people rushed around on the Underground, charging up escalators rather than letting themselves be carried up. 'Why would they have to get anywhere so quickly?' she asked. Guilty as charged—I am one of those who rushes around, tense and hurried. She is right: what is so important that it cannot wait?

Each one of us needs, deep in the core of our being, to spend time sharing 'the silence of eternity' described so well in the verse. I do not know many people who find this easy, but we should still keep trying. One aspect of this that I have discovered painfully (and then learnt that many others had discovered, too, from their own bitter experiences) is that it is extremely important we do not beat ourselves up when we fail to do this, for we will fail, inevitably, for much of the time. We should not be too harsh on ourselves. After all, God is not.

Perhaps that is what the mysterious phrase in the hymn 'interpreted by love' means. How else could we cope with either the silence—such a struggle for our distractable souls—or the eternity—so far beyond our limited horizons? We need love to interpret the sheer otherness of God.

Reflection

Pause a moment to think over how God might interpret your life by love.

RACHEL BOULDING

MATTHEW 6:6–8 (NRSV)

God knows our strain and stress

'But whenever you pray, go into your room and shut the door and pray to your Father who is in secret; and your Father who sees in secret will reward you. When you are praying, do not heap up empty phrases as the Gentiles do; for they think that they will be heard because of their many words. Do not be like them, for your Father knows what you need before you ask him.'

'Drop thy still dews of quietness, Till all our strivings cease; Take from our souls the strain and stress, And let our ordered lives confess The beauty of thy peace.' This seems more of a straightforward prayer or, rather, a heartfelt plea to God to help us in that silent prayer that we read about yesterday. If we are to have this quiet communion with the eternal, we must learn to be still.

The fact that this verse of the hymn, particularly the lines about 'ordered lives', usually provokes wry smiles or even feelings of guilt shows how difficult most of us find this. 'If only...', we think, as perhaps we imagine that all this is easier for others—ministers or nuns, perhaps. The fact is that it is hard for everyone. Easier for some than others, yes, but still hardly a doddle, even for them.

We must find ways to recover this hope, to turn to God in prayer and attend to his word, leaving to one side, if only briefly, the troubles of our lives. We must remember, too, that we cannot do this in our own strength; we can only direct our focus at God and keep on trying when we fall away. In this, we are at least choosing to devote some time to God. The words of the final line, and the tune, which embodies the beauty that it describes, can help us here. They can carry us towards hope and remind us of God. He is waiting for us and knows our needs, as Jesus reminds us in our passage today. God sees the good in us, despite all our inadequacies and struggling.

Reflection

What one thing could I do today to create a little space to feel God's presence and the beauty of his peace?

RACHEL BOULDING

Finding the Lord in stillness

And he said, Go forth, and stand upon the mount before the Lord. And, behold, the Lord passed by, and a great and strong wind rent the mountains, and brake in pieces the rocks before the Lord; but the Lord was not in the wind: and after the wind an earthquake; but the Lord was not in the earthquake: and after the earthquake a fire; but the Lord was not in the fire: and after the fire a still small voice.

'Breathe through the heats of our desire Thy coolness and thy balm; Let sense be dumb, let flesh retire; Speak through the earthquake, wind, and fire, O still, small voice of calm.' I find it funny that this hymn is so popular at weddings. It is really not appropriate for an occasion that is, in part, a celebration of 'the heats of our desire'. Again, though, as in verses 3 and 4, it is about the importance of turning aside from some aspects of our lives, towards God who is reaching out to us.

These areas of our lives are not necessarily bad in themselves. We need some of the striving of verse 4 and the desires of this verse, if only to survive on this planet, but I guess the hymn is saying that they should not dominate our existence. When we are able to recover our balance, it really will be 'balm'. We will discover the health of our souls, our wholeness and integrity. There is a long and venerable tradition of such turning away from the senses and finding God in the darkness. Obviously, God can be felt in images, music, emotions and our physical senses, but he can be approached in the absence of all these things, too.

This path to God, however we reach him, is what we are created to follow. As Augustine famously prayed, 'You have made us for yourself, O Lord, and our hearts are restless until they rest in you' (*Confessions*, I, 1).

Reflection

Can you turn aside, right now, and rest in the darkness with God?

RACHEL BOULDING

Known and loved by God

O Lord, thou hast searched me, and known me. Thou knowest my downsitting and mine uprising, thou understandest my thought afar off... Whither shall I go from thy spirit? or whither shall I flee from thy presence?... If I take the wings of the morning, and dwell in the uttermost parts of the sea; even there shall thy hand lead me, and thy right hand shall hold me. If I say, Surely the darkness shall cover me; even the night shall be light about me. Yea, the darkness hideth not from thee; but the night shineth as the day: the darkness and the light are both alike to thee.

The words of John Greenleaf Whittier's hymn that we have been considering these last few days outline a vision that is something to keep in front of us in the dark times, but also in the uninspiring, routine times. We need this hope before us. Crucially, these are not just words describing an unattainable ideal, so that we might feel we have to make an Olympic-style effort to grasp it. They describe a God who is always present, whether we acknowledge him or not, and who reaches out to help us.

Vitally, the music of the hymn helps to produce a situation and an atmosphere in which we can have some sense of this. The combination of words and music takes us to another place, beyond our own stresses and strivings. It carries us out of our messy, disorganised lives, towards the creator and sustainer of the universe. He is our loving father and 'Dear Lord', who cherishes humankind.

God knows us more deeply and thoroughly than we can imagine; he has probed our depths and our shallow dashing around. In the extremities and the middling places, he is waiting for us. As throughout this hymn, we are confronted by a challenge to make space for God, to carve out some time, however short and distracted, that is just for him. Knowing our limitations like no one else, God is patient with us.

Reflection

Try picking one or two lines of the hymn and praying them slowly. Mull over each word, conscious of God with you.

RACHEL BOULDING

Jesus in the upper room: John 14—15

Once again the season of Lent is almost upon us, providing an opportunity to reflect more intentionally on Jesus' life and death and consider our response to both before we celebrate his resurrection on Easter Sunday. Some will mark Lent by fasting from particular food or drink, forms of entertainment or lifestyle choices. Others might choose to read or set aside longer periods for prayer and contemplation. You might go to a church service on Ash Wednesday or else choose not to do anything different from usual.

As we embark on this period of the church's year, it is good to do so in the company of Jesus and his closest disciples in the upper room. While the first twelve chapters of John's Gospel might be particularly helpful to those exploring Christian faith, possibly not yet believers, the next four are highly relevant to those who know Jesus and are discovering the benefits and costs of discipleship.

By the end of chapter 13, Jesus has spoken about his betrayal by both Judas Iscariot and Peter and Judas has left. Jesus then addresses his words to the remaining disciples, offering comfort and encouragement, while also being clear about the challenges ahead. The disciples are desperate to understand, but their questions and Jesus' answers show just how little they grasp of who Jesus is, why he came and the significance of his departure. Perhaps understandably, the disciples are anxious about what will happen to them when Jesus has gone, seeking assurance, but not yet able to perceive how God will meet their needs.

At the time of writing, I am aware of loss in various forms among family and close friends, including chronic illness, terminal illness and relationship breakdown. We have been in our home for less than a year and our surroundings are yet to become familiar. We are aware of huge unsought change in the future. It can be a challenge to not 'let your hearts be troubled' (John 14:1). It often feels risky to believe that by trusting God and remaining in Christ, irrespective of our circumstances, our 'joy may be complete' (15:11). Yet, Jesus speaks to us now as he did to his disciples in the upper room. I pray, whatever your circumstances, that this will be your experience, too.

Lakshmi Jeffreys

Sunday 15 February

JOHN 14:1–3 (NRSV)

Belief and heartbeat

'Do not let your hearts be troubled. Believe in God, believe also in me. In my Father's house there are many dwelling places. If it were not so, would I have told you that I go to prepare a place for you? And if I go and prepare a place for you, I will come again and will take you to myself, so that where I am, there you may be also.'

Judas left the group to tell the authorities Jesus' whereabouts. Jesus informed the remaining disciples that Peter would betray him and that he himself would leave them. Not only will the person in the group apparently most loyal to Jesus actually be disloyal, but by the end of the evening none of them will have their master any longer. Surely anxiety in such circumstances is inevitable.

Among the common symptoms of anxiety are feelings of dread and an irregular heartbeat or palpitations. Perhaps that is why Jesus commands the disciples to not let their hearts be troubled. At that time, the heart was believed to be the centre of everything, including emotional, moral and intellectual existence, as well as physical life. Hence, Jesus is not simply saying, 'Calm down'; he wants them to trust God with their whole being in the midst of tremendous uncertainty and apprehension.

Fear is managed by providing information and reassurance. Jesus outlines to the disciples what he will do when he leaves them and reminds them to believe in God and in Jesus himself. He is going for their sake and will return to take them with him. This is enormously reassuring. There is purpose in Jesus' leaving: he is going to prepare a place for the disciples and will eventually accompany them there. Hearing that they are significant, even though Jesus will not be there, offers hope. They can continue to trust Jesus.

When hearts are racing and emotional, moral or intellectual life feels in turmoil, it can be helpful to stop and take heed of Jesus' words. In John's Gospel, belief in God is more than intellectual assent to the reality of a deity; it involves trust and action.

Reflection

What does it mean for me to believe in God?

LAKSHMI JEFFREYS

Navigational aid

> 'And you know the way to the place where I am going.' Thomas said to him, 'Lord, we do not know where you are going. How can we know the way?' Jesus said to him, 'I am the way, and the truth, and the life. No one comes to the Father except through me. If you know me, you will know my Father also. From now on you do know him and have seen him.'

An attested fact among those who know me is that I am not gifted in finding my way around. On hearing that, once again, I had got lost en route to somewhere, a former colleague drily remarked, 'Lakshmi needs a satnav to get round her kitchen!' As one who is at times unable to reach my destination without help, I have sympathy with Thomas' question: 'Lord, we do not know where you are going. How can we know the way?' (v. 5).

Jesus replies with some of the best-known words in scripture: 'I am the way, and the truth, and the life. No one comes to the Father except through me' (v. 6). In this statement, he reminds Thomas and the other disciples that the endpoint is God: Jesus himself is the road, the path, the way. He is not merely a signpost or even a satnav, but the one with, in and through whom we reach our ultimate destination. Jesus is the incarnate truth—God the Father made flesh. Jesus is the life, offering God's eternal life to all people who encounter him. Because of this, Jesus is the way for the disciples.

It is important for us to remember that Jesus is talking to his closest friends, people who have been with him for years. This statement is made to those who have encountered God, been alerted to signs of God's kingdom and experienced miracles. This is more than a simple doctrinal argument for exclusivity.

Perhaps we can consider Jesus' words in our own personal context, especially if we have a sense of knowing and being known by God and have experienced God's work in the world around us.

Reflection

What is the difference between the road and a navigational aid?
Which is Jesus for you?

LAKSHMI JEFFREYS

Seeing and knowing

Philip said to him, 'Lord, show us the Father, and we will be satisfied.' Jesus said to him, 'Have I been with you all this time, Philip, and you still do not know me? Whoever has seen me has seen the Father. How can you say, "Show us the Father"? Do you not believe that I am in the Father and the Father is in me?'

Philip's misunderstanding about Jesus is as profound as that of Thomas. Neither had seen beyond the human figure standing before them to the person himself—God in flesh. When we are with someone day in and day out, it is easy to miss the essence of who they are in the mundane routine. To be sure, the disciples had glimpsed God's glory in and through Jesus, but had yet to receive the full revelation that came with his death and resurrection. In time, they, like us, would be given insight through the Holy Spirit: as Paul puts it, God makes his light shine in our hearts to give us the knowledge of his glory displayed in the face of Christ (2 Corinthians 4:6).

Some years ago, a popular activity on Christian holidays for young people was 'Hunt the spy'. The leaders would disguise themselves and attempt to blend into the local town, while the young people in groups would try to identify them. If they found a leader, they would say a phrase and receive a response to show that they had been successful. Occasionally, 'hunters' were so busy trying to spot 'spies' that they would say the password to unsuspecting members of the public. Even though the leaders and young people had spent time together intensively, they did not always recognise the person outside their normal context.

It is easy to experience what we expect rather than realise who is actually there. How many times do we read words in the Bible yet do not pause to encounter the living God? It takes faith and enlightenment by the Holy Spirit to see Jesus as he is.

Prayer
Loving God, help me to see and reflect the glory in the face of Jesus.

LAKSHMI JEFFREYS

Believing

'The words that I say to you I do not speak on my own; but the Father who dwells in me does his works. Believe me that I am in the Father and the Father is in me; but if you do not, then believe me because of the works themselves. Very truly, I tell you, the one who believes in me will also do the works that I do and, in fact, will do greater works than these, because I am going to the Father. I will do whatever you ask in my name, so that the Father may be glorified in the Son. If in my name you ask me for anything, I will do it.'

Church leader Malcolm Duncan is also founder and director of an organisation committed to helping Christians and local churches engage with the wider community. He has said, 'Love always looks like something.' Real love is not a feeling but is offered and experienced in visible, tangible forms: spending time with someone who is lonely, feeding the hungry, fighting for justice alongside those who have no voice, bringing healing and forgiveness to a broken world.

Something similar applies to 'believing' in John's Gospel. It is not the cerebral occupation advocated in *Alice in Wonderland*, where the White Queen prides herself on having 'believed six impossible things before breakfast'. In fact, the word 'belief', an abstract concept, is never used in this Gospel. Instead, it is always 'believe'—an action. Since the disciples have been exhorted to believe in the Father and in Jesus, a relationship of trust is assumed. Perhaps a more accurate (if clumsier) translation might be, 'Trust me, I am in God and God is in me. If that seems too much, then have faith in what you have seen me do as a result of my obedience to God.'

Believing means trusting that Jesus' words and actions demonstrate the character of God, then behaving in a manner to show that this is true. Believing results in sharing the love and life of God in the world.

Prayer

Loving God, as I reflect on Jesus' words and actions, teach me to believe, trust and obey.

LAKSHMI JEFFREYS

The advocate of truth

'If you love me, you will keep my commandments. And I will ask the Father, and he will give you another Advocate, to be with you for ever. This is the Spirit of truth, whom the world cannot receive, because it neither sees him nor knows him. You know him, because he abides with you, and he will be in you.'

The condition that comes with the gift of the Holy Spirit is to keep God's commandments—the ultimate test of love for Jesus. The Holy Spirit will then come as an advocate. In legal parlance, an advocate supports a defendant in a trial. In fact, the disciples are promised the Spirit as *another* advocate, as they already have Jesus to defend them on earth. In time, he will continue to intercede for them (and us) in heaven.

Meanwhile, the Spirit is 'the Spirit of truth' (v. 17), the one who reveals the truth about Jesus to the world, just as Jesus revealed the truth about God to the world. Since 'the world' chose not to accept the truth about God, crucifying Jesus instead, only those who believe in Jesus (see yesterday's notes) will receive the Spirit and know the Spirit dwelling in them.

This picture of loving mutuality between God, Father, Son and Holy Spirit and encompassing those who accept Jesus, must have sounded extraordinary to the sad and frightened disciples in the upper room. Yet, in a matter of only weeks, these people would speak out about 'The Way', proclaiming Jesus risen from the dead.

Aged about five, our son was in a class where he and some other children were picked on by another pupil. Their experienced teacher worked with the children to sort out the situation and, shortly afterwards, our son was accused by the bully of being 'rubbish' at something. The response came back, 'I may not be so good at it, but I aren't rubbish!'

With someone to remind the disciples of reality, they had the courage to live in obedience to God. They knew that the Spirit of truth would support them as they spoke and lived the truth of God.

Prayer

*Spirit of truth, my Advocate for ever, live in me, that I may live
and speak the truth.*

LAKSHMI JEFFREYS

From existence to life

'I will not leave you orphaned; I am coming to you. In a little while the world will no longer see me, but you will see me; because I live, you also will live. On that day you will know that I am in my Father, and you in me, and I in you. They who have my commandments and keep them are those who love me; and those who love me will be loved by my Father, and I will love them and reveal myself to them.'

The word 'orphan' for many conjures images of abandonment, defencelessness and lack of belonging. A number of charities take toys and clothes to orphans in homes and orphanages overseas. A director of such an organisation spoke movingly of giving the children teddies. One child initially had no idea what to do with hers because she had never been given a toy before; another refused to let go, tightly hugging both the gift and the giver. A visible transformation took place as these children began to experience rich provision, that beyond barely sufficient food, clothing and shelter. The experience of being loved brought the children life.

Jesus promises not to leave his disciples as orphans. He will return to them after the resurrection, when they will see him even though the world around will want Jesus to be dead and will treat him as such. In his translation of the Bible, J.B. Phillips expresses it thus: 'You will see me, because I am really alive and you will be alive too.' Believing in Jesus, experiencing and expressing the love of God will bring life to the disciples.

Many people feel abandoned, defenceless, as if they do not belong, whether or not their parents are still alive. While God's love breaks through seemingly impenetrable boundaries, receiving and giving love involves practice and risk. The church today, as ever, needs to hear Jesus' words of consolation: we can see Jesus and know real life in order to keep God's commandments and share love and life with everyone we encounter.

Prayer

Pray for people who are orphans or feel abandoned and alone, that they may know love to bring them life.

LAKSHMI JEFFREYS

The choice to obey

Judas (not Iscariot) said to him, 'Lord, how is it that you will reveal yourself to us, and not to the world?' Jesus answered him, 'Those who love me will keep my word, and my Father will love them, and we will come to them and make our home with them. Whoever does not love me does not keep my words; and the word that you hear is not mine, but is from the Father who sent me.'

It is now Judas' turn to ask a question: 'How come you will make yourself known to us, but not to the world?' Once again, Jesus' answer appears oblique, but gets to the heart of what it means to belong to God. Jesus will be seen by anyone who chooses to share God's own life as Jesus has. To 'keep Jesus' words' is not the same as adhering to traffic rules or other codes of conduct. Obedience to God is to adopt God's pattern of life in everyday reality.

'Obedience' is not a comfortable word today. Neither are the related words—submission, respect, duty, deference. There is a justifiable reluctance to support many forms of submission when we hear horror stories of human slavery or various kinds of atrocities committed by those who were 'simply obeying orders'.

With Jesus, obedience is always coupled with love. Keeping God's word is a direct result of being loved by God and deciding to love God back. Love is never coercive, it is always a choice. The world at large chooses to ignore the God who created and loves everyone and everything; there is no desire to acknowledge, let alone submit to God. Equally, those who recognise and accept God's love for them in Jesus will hear and understand his words. As a result of being loved, we are able to obey because we know God wants to heal, reconcile and restore us, along with the entire creation, to wholeness. The result of obeying God is God being at home in us.

Reflection

We are most at home when we know we are loved and accepted and, therefore, how to behave in response to love.

LAKSHMI JEFFREYS

Facing the colossal with confidence

'Peace I leave with you; my peace I give to you. I do not give to you as the world gives. Do not let your hearts be troubled, and do not let them be afraid. You heard me say to you, "I am going away, and I am coming to you." If you loved me, you would rejoice that I am going to the Father, because the Father is greater than I. And now I have told you this before it occurs, so that when it does occur, you may believe.'

Throughout the Bible, the words 'Do not be afraid' are stated immediately preceding a colossal event, usually something alarming. The angel Gabriel told Mary not to be afraid before stating that she would bear God's son; other angels told the shepherds not to be afraid when they miraculously appeared during a nightshift in the hills around Bethlehem; Joshua was told not to be terrified as he was about to lead the people of God into the promised land. Jesus' disciples will have known scripture and history, so, as Jesus told them not to be afraid, they might have felt there was every reason to be scared stiff!

Jesus is not talking to people in 'the world'—those who do not believe and trust in God. He is talking to his closest friends and followers. They need not be afraid because Jesus is giving them the gift of peace. As has often been said, this peace is not an absence of conflict but, rather, the sense of security that comes from being in God. Peace for the Christian is the knowledge and experience that we are not alone in whatever we face. God is with us, so we can continue with confidence. Not only that, but Jesus has also told the disciples what to expect, so that they are not overwhelmed by events but are able to keep going with faith.

God's peace is not simply for the huge events in life. We can know Jesus with us in the everyday activities we sometimes fear but can tackle with trust.

Reflection

What huge or daily events make you afraid? Jesus is with you…

LAKSHMI JEFFREYS

Abide in the vine...

'I am the true vine, and my Father is the vine-grower. He removes every branch in me that bears no fruit. Every branch that bears fruit he prunes to make it bear more fruit. You have already been cleansed by the word that I have spoken to you. Abide in me as I abide in you. Just as the branch cannot bear fruit by itself unless it abides in the vine, neither can you unless you abide in me.'

In the Bible, the vine is a metaphor for the relationship between God and his people. Psalm 80 speaks of God having brought a vine out of Egypt before driving out the nations and planting it (v. 8). Meanwhile, Isaiah 5 offers a love song concerning a vineyard. The owner loved and tended the vine, but it produced only wild grapes. In the past, the vine—God's people—was not fruitful as God intended. However, Jesus speaks of himself as 'the true vine'. The people of God can at last have the life and love of God flowing through them without adhering to the Law and commandments—all that is required is 'abiding' in Jesus.

In John 14, Jesus spoke of God making his home with believers. In today's reading there is another image of abiding. The branch cannot exist independently of the vine, but, when attached to the main body of the vine, sap flows through the branch, sustaining life and enabling fruitfulness. Similarly, says Jesus, when we remain in him, the Holy Spirit brings us life and grows in us the fruit of the Spirit (Galatians 5:22–23).

Abiding in Jesus involves adopting the pattern of Jesus' life—spending time with God in prayer and Bible study, sharing bread and wine and worshipping with other Christians. As a result, we serve others and invite them to join us in the kingdom of God. Fruitfulness is more than developing the fruit of the Spirit; it means living in such a way that people around us become disciples of Jesus. Meanwhile, the image of pruning demonstrates how God cuts away all that is unproductive in life to increase our fruitfulness.

Prayer
Loving God, may I abide in you and be fruitful.

LAKSHMI JEFFREYS

... and only the vine!

'I am the vine, you are the branches. Those who abide in me and I in them bear much fruit, because apart from me you can do nothing. Whoever does not abide in me is thrown away like a branch and withers; such branches are gathered, thrown into the fire, and burned. If you abide in me, and my words abide in you, ask for whatever you wish, and it will be done for you. My Father is glorified by this, that you bear much fruit and become my disciples.'

Someone gave me this gardening tip: 'Grapevines are exuberant climbers, so if you plant one for its fruit you will need to keep it under control.' Considering the metaphor of Jesus as the vine and ourselves as branches, we are the part requiring discipline! Following yesterday's challenge of pruning, today's passage has a sobering image of branches being thrown away. There can be a superficial connection, too, so that the branch *appears* to be part of the vine, but does not have sap—the life—flowing through it. There is a façade of affiliation, but no real ability to bear fruit.

It is a challenge to not find our security and identity in possessions, education, money, popularity, intimate relationships, status or even a church or religious system, to name but a few, but if we choose to trust these aspects of life rather than Jesus, the consequences are drastic. Whoever does not abide in Jesus is thrown away. Apart from Jesus, the vine, a branch withers and dies. It is then fit only to be burned.

Before everyone panics, Jesus has more words of comfort. When we spend time with Jesus in prayer and read Bible passages (and perhaps even daily Bible reading notes!) we begin to imbibe his words. We are then in a position to ask God for what we want and need—and to receive it. While there is a clear warning about putting our trust and hope in things other than Jesus, we are also reminded of all the good that happens when we do stay with him.

Reflection

When we grow in discipleship, we bear fruit and, as we bear fruit, so we grow in discipleship.

LAKSHMI JEFFREYS

True joy

'As the Father has loved me, so I have loved you; abide in my love. If you keep my commandments, you will abide in my love, just as I have kept my Father's commandments and abide in his love. I have said these things to you so that my joy may be in you, and that your joy may be complete. This is my commandment, that you love one another as I have loved you.'

Someone else's good news can bring a mixture of emotions. Kate was delighted that her sister had qualified as a pilot and wept over her own mundane job. Joe was thrilled for his friends when they announced a baby was due, hiding his bitterness over his marriage break-up. Sam was overjoyed when he heard about the company's success and devastated that he was still on sick leave. In each case, joy for others is overwhelmed by the challenges of each person's own respective situation.

Jesus links joy with love. Because Jesus loves the disciples—and indeed the world—he will endure the cross before being raised from death by God. After the resurrection, Jesus' closest followers will remember his words and their joy will be complete. This joy is not 'looking on the bright side' or 'putting on a brave face' and feeling slightly better as a result. As joy is a product of love, so love in the upper room is linked to obedience and sacrifice. The remarkable feature of joy is that Jesus' friends will know it because of—rather than in spite of—their obedience. Moreover, their joy will be complete in and through sacrifice.

Similarly, the psalmist, surrounded by the enemy but knowing safety in God's care, offers 'sacrifices with shouts of joy' (Psalm 27:6). Those who know something of abiding in Jesus will echo this approach to worship. Joy is independent of personal circumstances. Just as God's peace overcomes fear, so joy prevails over suffering when we have God's perspective. There is an unexpected outpouring of thankfulness and maybe even a song.

Prayer

Pray slowly through Psalm 27, pausing to reflect on your circumstances and inviting the Holy Spirit to bring God's perspective. Can you offer 'sacrifices with shouts of joy… sing and make melody to the Lord' (v. 6)?

LAKSHMI JEFFREYS

Love and friendship

'No one has greater love than this, to lay down one's life for one's friends. You are my friends if you do what I command you. I do not call you servants any longer, because the servant does not know what the master is doing; but I have called you friends, because I have made known to you everything that I have heard from my Father. You did not choose me but I chose you. And I appointed you to go and bear fruit, fruit that will last, so that the Father will give you whatever you ask him in my name. I am giving you these commands so that you may love one another.'

It is easy to believe we offer sacrificial love. Unfortunately, we are not always aware of who is being sacrificed! C.S. Lewis highlights this in *The Screwtape Letters* (1942): 'She's the sort of woman who lives for others—you can tell the others by their hunted expression.' Expression of loving service can be patronising. One client at a soup kitchen was overheard to say, 'These young people are kind but I hate being "worked among"!'

When Jesus speaks of love and friendship between the disciples and himself, he is not referring to a relationship of equals. While he was completely human, he was still completely God, hence the statement, surprising to modern ears, 'You are my friends if you do what I command you.' Most of us would bristle at being ordered around by so-called friends! In our relationship with God, however, there is both intimacy—knowing through Jesus whatever God reveals—and duty. We and all disciples of Jesus have been loved and chosen and appointed to live in a way that brings God's love, life and choice to others. Out of the love and friendship, intimacy and self-revelation we encounter with God comes the ability to love others as Jesus loves. This love is self-giving because there is nothing to prove or demand; anything we need will be given when we ask our Father God in Jesus' name. We cannot earn or lose God's love; it is a gift.

Reflection

Friendship with, and obedience to, our creator God leads to real self-sacrificial love.

LAKSHMI JEFFREYS

Inevitable conflict

'If the world hates you, be aware that it hated me before it hated you. If you belonged to the world, the world would love you as its own. Because you do not belong to the world, but I have chosen you out of the world—therefore the world hates you. Remember the word that I said to you, "Servants are not greater than their master." If they persecuted me, they will persecute you; if they kept my word, they will keep yours also. But they will do all these things to you on account of my name, because they do not know him who sent me.'

The inevitable result of the outpouring of God's love in the world is conflict. Jesus knew what it was to be hated. In a few weeks' time we shall recall the poignancy of the Last Supper, the agony of Gethsemane and the apparent finality of the cross. Jesus would send his disciples into the world and the opposition he faced would be transferred to them. No one could say they had not been warned!

Why should self-sacrificial love lead to persecution? Perhaps it is because love that is not self-seeking is, counter-intuitively, enormously threatening. Power in the world is usually exercised by means of manipulation, bullying or at least highlighting, if not exploiting, differences in wealth, status or education. A person—or a community—seeking simply to serve brings to light injustice and evil. As it says earlier in John's Gospel (3:19–20), 'the light has come into the world, and people loved darkness rather than light because their deeds were evil. For all who do evil hate the light and do not come to the light, so that their deeds may not be exposed.'

Those who choose to respond to God's love and live in the light will no longer be accepted by a world choosing to stay in darkness. Yet, the way against the resulting evil, persecution and hatred is through constant love, which comes from the Father, is mediated by Jesus and empowered by the Holy Spirit.

Reflection

Expression of God's love leads to conflict. Expression of God's love is the only lasting answer to conflict.

LAKSHMI JEFFREYS

What is to come

'If I had not come and spoken to them, they would not have sin; but now they have no excuse for their sin. Whoever hates me hates my Father also. If I had not done among them the works that no one else did, they would not have sin. But now they have seen and hated both me and my Father. It was to fulfil the word that is written in their law, "They hated me without a cause." When the Advocate comes, whom I will send to you from the Father, the Spirit of truth who comes from the Father, he will testify on my behalf. You also are to testify because you have been with me from the beginning.'

This is the second time the Holy Spirit is mentioned as an advocate. The word in Greek means 'one called alongside to help and plead for us'. The passage speaks about testifying and continues the legal language of the previous chapter. Those who hate Jesus, and, consequently, God the Father, have testified against themselves. They have seen Jesus; they know the difference between God's way and the way of the world and they still choose to ignore God, which is the root of sin.

The injustice of a world that hates Jesus without cause is combated by the Spirit of truth. The Holy Spirit gives disciples, then and now, the words and means to bear witness to the saving love of Jesus. The Holy Spirit does more than simply act as a lawyer, pointing out the truth, however. As Brother Ramon wrote in the notes in *New Daylight* for 8 November 1999, 'The Holy Spirit not only comforts us, but fortifies, encourages and inspires us to face the dark power of the enemy.'

As we finish these days in the upper room, we do so with the promise of the Holy Spirit. Life would get much harder for the disciples and, indeed, life will not always be easy for us. There would be active hatred and persecution alongside pain and suffering, but, with the assurance of Jesus' love and the promise of the Holy Spirit, they—and we—continue in faith until the joy and hope of Easter.

Prayer

Come, Holy Spirit!

LAKSHMI JEFFREYS

Don't forget to renew your annual subscription to *New Daylight*! If you enjoy the notes, why not also consider giving a gift subscription to a friend or member of your family?

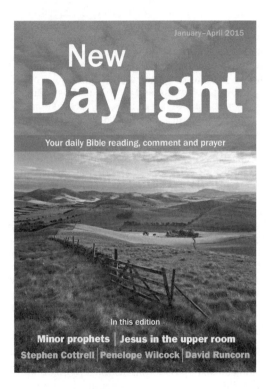

You will find subscription order forms on pages 156 and 157.
New Daylight is also available from your local Christian bookshop.

The way of humility

'See, your king comes to you, righteous and victorious, lowly and riding on a donkey, on a colt, the foal of a donkey' (Zechariah 9:9, NIV).

'The Word became flesh and made his dwelling among us. We have seen his glory, the glory of the one and only Son, who came from the Father, full of grace and truth' (John 1:14, NIV).

'[She] wrapped him in swaddling clothes, and laid him in a manger; because there was no room for them in the inn' (Luke 2:7, KJV).

Do you know the famous and beautiful song 'Panis Angelicus'? Written by Thomas Aquinas, set to music by César Franck, it describes the Eucharist: *'Panis Angelicus fit panis hominum; Dat panis cœlicus figuris terminum; O res mirabilis! Manducat Dominum Pauper, pauper, servus et humilis.'*

Bread of angels becomes human bread, giving bread of heaven limited form. Astonishing business! The poor, the enslaved, the humble, consume the Lord. The Eucharist has been, since earliest days, the miraculous, transformative heart of Christian faith and worship. Aquinas here probes the mystery of this living core and finds it to be humility—the transcendent, omnipotent supremacy of God become so small and simple as to be bread for the lowliest of humankind.

Charles Wesley, contemplating the same humility in the incarnation, wrote in his hymn 'Let earth and heaven combine': 'The incarnate Deity, our God contracted to a span, incomprehensibly made man.'

The way of humility, then, is not so much something required of us by God, as something intrinsic to God's very nature. Drawing near him at all, touching his life with ours, is encountering the profound humility of his self-offering. The way of humility is the only way to become like Jesus, because humble is what Jesus is.

'Humility' has its roots in the Latin for 'earth'—*humus*. 'Human', from the Latin *humanus*, grows from the same root. A humble person is close to the earth—lowly—and this is natural, because we are formed from the earth, which is what the Hebrew *Adam* and Latin *humanus* both imply. So, the way of humility is not second nature, but the substance from which our life arises—innate. To the extent we have strayed from it, we are lost.

Penelope Wilcock

Not more but less

> Will the Lord be pleased with thousands of rams, or with ten thousands of rivers of oil? shall I give my firstborn for my transgression, the fruit of my body for the sin of my soul? He hath shewed thee, O man, what is good; and what doth the Lord require of thee, but to do justly, and to love mercy, and to walk humbly with thy God?

When I put my mind to the question of what God thinks of me, I usually worry that I am not enough for him—not good enough or kind enough. I feel ashamed of how little time I spend in prayer and studying scripture.

Now, holding the Bible open in my hands, looking into these words of the prophet Micah as I would look into a deep pool, trying to perceive what is real, I wonder if perhaps all these years I have been looking through the wrong end of the binoculars; maybe God is asking of me not more, but less.

Micah draws a picture of life so simple and plain that even a child could do it. He outlines a scenario in which the grand gesture, the extravagant sacrifice and all the rest are not only unnecessary but also actually get in the way. He suggests that, instead of all the huffing and puffing of attainment, we choose unadorned honesty and integrity—fair, balanced, orderly justice. He proposes that, in our dealings with others, we choose to be kind—to temper the wind to the shorn lamb, showing loving mercy. He also invites us not to a life of grand achievement but a path of littleness, walking humbly with our God.

Although this way of life seems small and unassuming, it is (as estate agents say) deceptively spacious. It makes time for reflection and prayer, for noticing how others feel; it is a beautiful path.

Prayer

In your astonishing humility, kind and loving God, you consent to share my human journey. In Jesus I can see the face of who you really are. Give me the grace to walk with you this day, simply, without affectation, only sharing with you the face of who I really am.

PENELOPE WILCOCK

Ducking under

Jews demand signs and Greeks look for wisdom, but we preach Christ crucified: a stumbling-block to Jews and foolishness to Gentiles, but to those whom God has called, both Jews and Greeks, Christ the power of God and the wisdom of God. For the foolishness of God is wiser than human wisdom, and the weakness of God is stronger than human strength. Brothers and sisters, think of what you were when you were called. Not many of you were wise by human standards; not many were influential; not many were of noble birth. But God chose the foolish things of the world to shame the wise; God chose the weak things of the world to shame the strong.

When I first became a Christian, at the age of 15, I discovered with delight the *Fioretti*—tales about Francis and his first followers, the beginnings of the Franciscan order. Francis used to speak of being in love with Lady Poverty and gave his whole life to pursuing humility and simplicity—the naked, barefoot gospel. A mystic and a man of prayer, he could often be found rapt in adoration of his beloved Jesus, who gave up everything for our salvation.

Like all who walk a path of faith and personal holiness, Francis was plagued by temptations. At first he tried to overcome them, struggling to be stronger than they were. Then his Lord showed him a different way. He learned that, instead of trying to pump himself up with the strength to overcome, by accepting his own weakness he could become small enough to duck underneath the temptation. He learned to resist sin by the sheer power of insignificance!

Much of our own sin is about dissension or ambition, wanting power or position, coveting attention, achievement and status. Instead of struggling vainly to overcome, we can learn from Francis to become small enough to slip underneath it and wriggle free.

Prayer

Gracious God, I am moved and amazed that, from the magnificence of the heavens you stoop down to me, creature of dust, finitude, frailty, and pick me up and carry me in the immensity of your love. May I always remember to stay small enough for your love to carry me home.

Penelope Wilcock

The first creed

Be humble towards one another... The attitude you should have is the one that Christ Jesus had: He always had the nature of God, but he did not think that by force he should try to remain equal with God. Instead of this, of his own free will he gave up all he had, and took the nature of a servant. He... appeared in human likeness. He was humble and walked the path of obedience all the way to death.

'Jesus is Lord', motto of the World Council of Churches, is thought to be the first ever Christian creed. We find reference to it in the epistles of the New Testament—for example, Romans 10:9 (NIV): 'If you declare with your mouth, "Jesus is Lord," and believe in your heart that God raised him from the dead, you will be saved' and Philippians 2:10–11 (NIV): 'At the name of Jesus every knee should bow, in heaven and on earth and under the earth, and every tongue acknowledge that Jesus Christ is Lord, to the glory of God the Father.'

I used to think the creed 'Jesus is Lord' was the place where the church began to go wrong—setting as the foundation of our credal statements not the love Jesus himself said would be the hallmark of discipleship but an assertion of dominance and supremacy. When I thought about it more deeply, however, I began to understand what this statement of faith is teaching. It is Jesus, who never used force, coercion or violence but chose the way of the humble servant, who is Lord. There is an old Chinese saying that 'the sea is king of a hundred streams because it lies below them'. Like water, humble, useful and clean, finding its way round the rocks without fighting or blaming, patiently wearing away the obstacles in its path, the way of the kingdom is gentle, humble. This, not overbearing dominance, is true overcoming, because it involves achieving mastery over oneself.

Prayer

Thank you, O God, that, though we tremble before your dread might, you delight to surprise us with your humble love made known to us in Jesus.

PENELOPE WILCOCK

2 Kings 5:13–14 (NIV)

Accepting a humble role

Naaman's servants went to him and said, 'My father, if the prophet had told you to do some great thing, would you not have done it? How much more, then, when he tells you, "Wash and be cleansed"!' So he went down and dipped himself in the Jordan seven times, as the man of God had told him, and his flesh was restored and became clean like that of a young boy.

The Covenant Prayer features in Methodist churches at the start of each new year. It is an unreserved self-offering and dedication for Christian service. Starting with the words, 'I am no longer my own but yours', it makes such commitments as, 'Let me be employed for you or laid aside for you, exalted for you or brought low for you.' The preamble to the prayer starts: 'Christ has many services to be done. Some are easy, others are difficult.'

When Methodists pray these words, they do so with trepidation. Who knows what God may ask of them? Yet, oddly, it is often not the great or demanding responsibilities that disciples find hard to accept, but the overlooked, insignificant jobs, such as staying home to babysit while someone else goes out in the night as a street pastor; putting out (and clearing away) the chairs and tables for a meeting at which someone else will be the speaker; doing the laundry and getting the groceries so someone else is free to be an evangelist.

This was Naaman's struggle. Ready to face tough challenges requiring noble character, he was unprepared to stomach the humiliation of being unimportant and ignored, left to carry out an unexceptional assignment, by himself, without encouragement or congratulation.

We dream of being heroes, taking a starring role, but the truth is God needs many, many pilgrims to walk his way of humility, ensuring that the torch of the gospel is carried in our own generation by our faithfulness in the simple, ordinary tasks.

Prayer

Give me the simplicity and humility of Christ, O God of grace, that I may be content with whatever you ask of me and whatever position you assign me, no matter how lowly and insignificant that may be.

PENELOPE WILCOCK

Resting in humility

Jesus said 'I praise you, Father, Lord of heaven and earth, because you have hidden these things from the wise and learned, and revealed them to little children... Come to me, all you who are weary and burdened, and I will give you rest. Take my yoke upon you and learn from me, for I am gentle and humble in heart, and you will find rest for your souls. For my yoke is easy and my burden is light.'

Understandably, we think of humility as hard, as a real challenge! All of us want to be important, to be congratulated and praised, have people make a fuss of us: it is only human nature. We glow and flourish when we are affirmed and appreciated and God made us to be like that when he created us to live in relationship with others. So, when we contemplate humility—taking a back seat, willingly accepting others disregarding us, even deriding us—naturally, we feel daunted.

Though parts of the way of humility are indeed uphill and stony, some aspects of the journey are beautiful, refreshing and peaceful.

When Jesus makes a promise, he is not deceiving us with empty words: we can absolutely trust what he says. Here he assures us that, if we are willing to be yoked together with him in gentleness and humility, with the simplicity of children, we will find rest for our souls.

It is not learning to be humble, but constantly striving for perfection, seeking attention, coveting the first place, that really wears us out. We are not made for incessant competition and anxiety about achievement, the stress of which can make us physically ill. Humility is about being content with who we are and what God has given us. That brings peace and opens in our hearts a wellspring of gratitude for all the blessings we need humility to recognise.

Prayer

Dearest Lord, when I feel afraid to take the way of humility, when I am scared of the cost, encourage me with your vision of peace and gentleness, restore in me the childlike simplicity of faith and remind me that I will be walking in step with Jesus, all the way home.

PENELOPE WILCOCK

Do you know what I have done to you?

After Jesus had washed their feet, he put his outer garment back on and returned to his place at the table. 'Do you understand what I have just done to you?' he asked. 'You call me Teacher and Lord, and it is right that you do so, because that is what I am. I, your Lord and Teacher, have just washed your feet. You, then, should wash one another's feet.'

Jeannie Gibson, a long-term employee with the Bahamas Ministry of Tourism, writes in *LiveLiving* magazine (27 June 2013), 'The simplest definition of humility is "not being focused on self".'

She tells of a time when, new to a job in Chicago, she was at the staff Christmas dinner when gifts were given out. She felt humiliated to receive two tins of conch chowder (a soup that is a Bahamian speciality), when others had prettier, more exciting presents. Embarrassed, she assumed the gift was given to her condescendingly as she was a single mother. Long afterwards the memory still made her hot with shame. Then, one day, she had an 'Oh, I see!' moment. She remembered a conversation with the colleague who had given her the gift, in which she had mentioned how homesick she felt for the Bahamas. In choosing that gift, this colleague had intended the best thing of all—a taste of home. Jeannie had completely missed the point of what her friend had done for her. She had been too wrapped up in her own insecurities to see her colleague's kindness.

Jesus, too, had trouble with friends who missed the point, too anxious about their own position to follow his lead in practising humility.

Jeannie concludes: 'Humility, often not easily achieved, allows one to be comfortable for each situation and circumstance as necessary.' She got the point that Jesus wanted us to see: humility sets us free, dissolves the tension of insecurity. When we are content to take the lowest place, not embarrassed to fail or look foolish, our relationships improve, our inner peace is restored and we find ourselves having a whole lot more fun.

Prayer

Grant us, O God, the humility to let go of preoccupation with status and image; set us free to be like Jesus.

PENELOPE WILCOCK

Only me and God

'The tax collector stood at a distance and would not even raise his face to heaven, but beat on his breast and said, "God, have pity on me, a sinner!" I tell you,' said Jesus, 'the tax collector, and not the Pharisee, was in the right with God when he went home. For all who make themselves great will be humbled, and all who humble themselves will be made great.'

There is a voice of discontentment in most of us, always wanting to be bigger and better. Inflation by comparison, you might call it. Not content with ourselves as we are, we boast of being the only species who can do this or that thing, how humanity alone has such-and-such an attribute. How pitiful that we attempt aggrandisement by making comparisons with the giraffe, the woodlouse or the mealworm.

Our passage today is part of a longer story in which a Pharisee, his glance falling on a tax collector, gives thanks to God for not being like him (vv. 11–12). He recites the catalogue of his own considerable virtues, adding to the height of his achievement by comparing himself with the dirt-beneath-his-feet taxman.

In his journal *Markings* (1964), Dag Hammarskjöld, the second Secretary-General of the United Nations, wrote of comparing himself with other people, sometimes thinking himself better than others, then concluding, 'Why should you be? Either you are what you can be, or you are not—like other people.'

Our tax collector, who, Jesus says, went home justified, makes no attempt to compare himself with the Pharisee or anyone else. He acknowledges his own unimpressive reality without trying to boost it by drawing attention to the shortcomings of others. It seems this is what God wants of us—that we have the humility simply to be ourselves, face-to-face with the Father who knows and loves us.

Prayer
Ah, creator God! Where could I hide from you? Even if I stand behind someone else, you see that and smile. When I try to distract you with others' faults, you still look steadily at me. Hide-and-seek God, have mercy on me, a sinner, in all my insecurity, my foolish pride.

PENELOPE WILCOCK

Leaving omniscience to God

> Accept the one whose faith is weak, without quarrelling over disputable matters. One person's faith allows them to eat anything, but another, whose faith is weak, eats only vegetables. The one who eats everything must not treat with contempt the one who does not, and the one who does not eat everything must not judge the one who does, for God has accepted them. Who are you to judge someone else's servant?

Jesus came out with the devastating remark that you cannot follow him unless you give up everything you have (Luke 14:33). We usually think of this in terms of material wealth—money and possessions. The idea that Jesus might try to part us from our hard-earned assets is very unnerving.

One of the treasures we hold most dear, however, is not a tangible thing at all, but the sweet satisfaction of knowing we are right—and making sure everyone else knows it, too!

In today's passage, Paul tackles the matter of dietary scruples. Even if we were not brought up in a religion that has food rules, what we eat can still be a source of moral contention: ethical farming, Fairtrade and nutritional health create controversy, especially in an age when obesity has reached epidemic proportions.

Paul is not asking us to ignore the promptings of our conscience in our own choices, nor to make helpful information unavailable, but to respect the choices of other people, and bear in mind that (yes, shocking, I know!) we may even, occasionally, be wrong.

He makes the point that, in the end, we are answerable not to each other but to God. We forbear from judging because we have the humility to acknowledge the dignity inherent in our brothers and sisters, for they, like us, are servants of the most high God.

Prayer

Give me the humility, gracious God, to respect the moral choices of others, even when they do not reflect my own. Help me to listen carefully for your Spirit's whisper, to trust my brothers and sisters in Christ to hear your word for themselves and to remember that sometimes I simply get it wrong.

PENELOPE WILCOCK

ROMANS 12:2–3 (KJV)

Honest truth

> Be not conformed to this world: but be ye transformed by the
> renewing of your mind, that ye may prove what is that good, and
> acceptable, and perfect, will of God. For I say, through the grace
> given unto me, to every man that is among you, not to think of
> himself more highly than he ought to think; but to think soberly,
> according as God hath dealt to every man the measure of faith.

It is not luck or circumstances that determine the quality of our lives,
but the way we think, our attitudes and habits of mind. Even the most
unpromising beginnings can be nurtured into something wonderful,
just as a fire can be started from a tiny spark and a big leafy plant can
grow from a little seed.

So it is that Paul says we do not have to follow the crowd; learning
to think differently will absolutely transform us.

Very often, preachers will quote the inspiring words of our passage
today and leave it there, not going on to the next bit that encourages us
to have the humility to assess ourselves realistically. Humble souls are
ready to acknowledge their limitations and frailties, of course, but will
also make a balanced and honest evaluation of their gifts and graces.

All through the Bible runs the theme of the people of God. We are
called to belonging, to be part of a community from which we draw
sustenance and support and to which we each make our unique contribution. Wisely appraising my strengths and weaknesses helps me discern the niche that only I can fill. This process is helped when we have
the humility to listen to others when they comment on our input. As
Frederick Buechner put it, 'The place God calls you to is the place
where your deep gladness and the world's deep hunger meet' (*Wishful
Thinking*, HarperCollins, 1993).

Prayer

*Father God, you watch over your people, drawing us always closer
to you and to one another. Help me to find the place you created
me for, where I can make the best possible contribution to the
household of God, so that nothing I can offer is wasted and
nothing I do hinders the ministry of others.*

PENELOPE WILCOCK

His mother's son

He hath regarded the lowliness of his handmaiden. For behold, from henceforth all generations shall call me blessed. For he that is mighty has magnified me and holy is his name. And his mercy is on them that fear him throughout all generations. He hath shewed strength with his arm: he hath scattered the proud in the imagination of their hearts. He hath put down the mighty from their seat and hath exalted the humble and meek.

Maybe at some point in your life you have sung the children's hymn that starts with the line 'Gentle Jesus meek and mild'. It is a lovely hymn and makes an excellent lullaby for a restless infant, too, but you do have to wonder just how much the author had read about Jesus! His mother's famous song, known down the centuries as the Magnificat (Luke 1:48–52), is a red hot political protest that could strip paint at thirty metres and the powers that be had good reason for their keenness to see her son nailed firmly to a cross.

What does that mean about our preconceptions concerning humility? Mary's song speaks of being raised up, of being exalted from under the might of the oppressor to a position of freedom, where the poor and downtrodden could hold their heads high.

When we describe someone as humble, we tend to imagine a soft-voiced, non-confrontational individual with a downward gaze and conciliatory manner. Mary's 'lowly handmaiden', though, is the type who stands up straight, looks you right in the eye and backs down for nobody! Reading the words of her son Jesus in the Gospels may give us cause here and there to rethink our ideas about 'gentle Jesus meek and mild'.

So, in what is their humility vested, if not in apologetic appeasement? Zechariah (4:6, KJV) put it in a nutshell when he said, 'Not by might, nor by power, but by my spirit, saith the Lord'. The humility of Jesus and Mary is all about standing firm because they trust in God.

Prayer

Rock of Ages, God of my salvation, in quietness and humility may I show my strength. I do not need to brag and need prove nothing, only trust in you.

PENELOPE WILCOCK

He came in great humility

And the angel said unto [the shepherds], Fear not: for, behold, I bring you good tidings of great joy, which shall be to all people. For unto you is born this day in the city of David a Saviour, which is Christ the Lord. And this shall be a sign unto you; Ye shall find the babe wrapped in swaddling clothes, lying in a manger.

The point of a sign is to encapsulate the essence of what it is about. Think of the 'danger of death' sign on the barred gate of an electrical installation, showing lightning zapping a fallen man. Think of the Highway Code with its many signs—a road narrowing, falling rocks, pedestrians—any number of minimalistic images conveying at a glance what lies ahead.

Then there is the British Sign Language of the deaf community, with its vivid depictions of words and phrases. There are famous logos, too, such as McDonalds, Citroën, His Master's Voice—all fulfilling the function of a sign by making what they represent immediately recognisable. I wonder what you might choose as the sign of your life?

I am fairly certain there is no PR company in the entire world that would have come up with this sign for God incarnate—a baby wrapped in swaddling clothes, lying in a manger. To us, frankly, that does not communicate 'God'. So begins the struggle at the heart of Jesus' teaching ministry—reinventing from first principles our ideas about power, leadership and what it means to be the Messiah. His words in the Gospels challenge our preconceptions and expectations, tearing up the old script and beginning again. Leadership, says Jesus, is about responsibility, sacrifice, service and, yes, humility.

It all began here, with this sign—a homeless baby in an animal's feed trough, bound in swaddling bands. Unable to speak, reason, command; utterly vulnerable. A well-swaddled baby can't even move! And this, says the angel, is the sign of God's presence on earth.

Prayer

God of surprises, you turned our ideas upside down when you came to us in Jesus. Give us grace to learn this improbable way—and the courage to follow it.

PENELOPE WILCOCK

MARK 15:17–20 (NIV)

The king of heaven

[The soldiers] put a purple robe on [Jesus], then twisted together a crown of thorns and set it on him. And they began to call out to him, 'Hail, king of the Jews!' Again and again they struck him on the head with a staff and spat on him. Falling on their knees, they paid homage to him. And when they had mocked him, they took off the purple robe and put his own clothes on him. Then they led him out to crucify him.

This passage shows us, almost more vividly and graphically than we can bear, one of the central characteristics of humility: it is not domination of others but the strength to attain mastery over oneself.

A variety of psychological experiments, carried out mainly during the 20th century, made it depressingly clear that humans are social beings, to the extent that we will follow the herd, obey the commands of our leaders and fulfil the expectations of our peer group, even when that means cruelly inflicting suffering on people and animals in our power. The soldiers in this painful episode are behaving normally—doing the kinds of thing people always do. No doubt we have done something similar ourselves, jeering at a safe target, being mean to someone who is powerless or down on their luck.

Bullying, we know, is an indication of weakness; the bully is always afraid. These bullies, too, are part of a bullying chain of command, but they were mistaken in assuming that Jesus was in their power. On the contrary, they were in his. The power to bless or curse, to work miracles and alter physical conditions, was part of everyday life for Jesus. What we witness here is the strength of humility, which meant he refrained from self-preservation, vilification and even complaint, for the sake of making it possible for God to fulfil in him the task he came for—the reconciliation of creation, the salvation of the world. It makes the power of the bully look very small.

Prayer

For our heartlessness and cruelty, Father forgive us. Give us the strength of humility to attain mastery over ourselves, so that compassion and reconciliation may flow through our lives and we may follow Jesus.

PENELOPE WILCOCK

Leaving room for God to give

'When someone invites you to a wedding feast, do not sit down in the best place... Instead, when you are invited, go and sit in the lowest place, so that your host will come to you and say, "Come on up, my friend, to a better place." This will bring you honour in the presence of all the other guests. For those who make themselves great will be humbled, and those who humble themselves will be made great.'

A familiar phrase as a birthday approaches is, 'What do you give a man (or woman) who has everything?' Usually, all kinds of suggestions follow, geared to tempting the jaded appetite of someone who has too much. Poverty still abounds but our consumer society has created weariness and lassitude in those who have done everything and bought everything.

The astringency of humility brings peace and relief. A simple, humble, frugal lifestyle invites quietness and contentment. Time in silence and solitude allows the soul to settle, making space for reflection.

Best of all, simplicity and humility make room again for love. The man or woman who no longer has everything will regain the joy of eagerly awaited birthdays and Christmas when, once more, hand-knitted scarves and gloves really *are* just what they wanted, and a home-made fruitcake with a small truckle of cheese are stowed away in the larder as treasure.

To those who walk a quiet path, living in lowliness, comes the delight of unexpected recognition, the exciting upgrade to first class, the 'Who? Me?' of being acknowledged and rewarded. I realised when my children were young that one of the many advantages of a low income is that you have more treats than rich people. One of the joys of humility is making room in your life to hope, receive, be delighted, allowing someone else the privilege of affirming you and not always having to be the one in charge.

Prayer

O God of blessing, you love to pour out on us the abundance of your kindness. Give us grace to live with such simplicity, such humility, that our lives have space to receive all that you long to give.

Penelope Wilcock

The Servant King

Jesus called [his disciples] together and said, 'You know that those who are regarded as rulers of the Gentiles lord it over them, and their high officials exercise authority over them. Not so with you. Instead, whoever wants to become great among you must be your servant, and whoever wants to be first must be slave of all. For even the Son of Man did not come to be served, but to serve, and to give his life as a ransom for many.'

This passage has special significance. Of the four evangelists, Mark wrote his Gospel first and, in it, he tackled a task we should not underestimate—redefining leadership. In particular, he shows how Jesus not so much reinterpreted the role of Messiah as turned conventional thinking upside down.

The Jewish people were looking for a Messiah to usher in a new era like the golden age of King David, someone who would be the glorious leader of a triumphant people. Jesus saw things differently.

Mark's Gospel starts with the statement that Jesus is the Son of God. Next follow several chapters about the miracles of Jesus that cause people to ask, 'Who is this?' Then comes a central block of teaching in which Jesus challenges traditional thinking about what it means to be the Messiah. Once that has been completed, Mark turns to the great narrative of the passion, culminating in the Roman centurion, representative of the great mass of people beyond the bounds of Judaism, affirming, 'Surely this man was the Son of God' (Mark 10:45). This *man*—not a king on his throne, but a beaten, tortured man nailed to a cross.

Our passage is the nub of Jesus' teaching concerning reinterpreting the role of Messiah, his concluding words to the central block of teaching: 'the Son of Man did not come to be served, but to serve, and to give his life as a ransom for many' (15:39). He saw the role of Messiah as servant-king, crowned with the unexpected glory and strength of humility.

Prayer

By your miraculous power, O God, give me the grace to follow Jesus, to choose the way of humility that he walked every day.

PENELOPE WILCOCK

Jesus in the upper room: John 16—17

For the next two weeks our daily readings will be taken from chapters 16 and 17 of John's Gospel. Of the four Gospels John's is perhaps the hardest to divide up in this way. He weaves themes together very intricately. His style is poetic, richly layered with meaning, and his train of thought is not always obvious to contemporary readers. These two chapters are good examples of this. It is easy to get a kind of theological indigestion if you try to take in too much at once.

A good place to start might be to read through these chapters in one go. As you read, do not stop to ponder particular words or phrases. Think of it as stepping back to get the bigger picture or standing at a vantage point from which to take in the sweep of a whole landscape and its broadest features. When you do this, what stands out for you? Are there particular words, phrases or images that you notice? What is the overall mood of these chapters? Do you sense their main purpose and intention? Do not worry about understanding at this point. The first task is just to notice and take time looking. You might repeat this at the end of each week.

These chapters are very important in the overall shape of John's Gospel because they come immediately before the betrayal, trial and crucifixion of Jesus. Here, on the threshold of his death and resurrection, they offer a kind of theological summary of the significance of Jesus. This is revealed first in his ministry to his disciples (chapter 16) and then through his prayer to the Father (chapter 17).

While I was writing these notes, my wife was adjusting to wearing new glasses. They are varifocals and she found them quite disorientating at first. With a slight tilt of the head, the focus shifts between close, medium and long distance vision. Reading John is a bit like that: the focal length keeps changing. We will begin by focusing closely on the disciples. Their vision is limited, too. But look up just a little. This story is cosmic—and the key to it all is Jesus.

David Runcorn

Remember

'I have said these things to you to keep you from stumbling. They will put you out of the synagogues. Indeed, an hour is coming when those who kill you will think that by doing so they are offering worship to God. And they will do this because they have not known the Father or me. But I have said these things to you so that when their hour comes you may remember that I told you about them.'

There is a loving, careful concern running through this passage. Jesus wants his disciples to be as prepared as possible for the time of his 'departure' (see 13:1). He also wants them to be ready for the times when following him will lead, as he knows it will, to violent opposition and even death. This is tough wisdom for tough times. The message is not 'When they try to hurt you I will stop them', but, 'When it happens, remember I told you it would be so'.

So, who are the 'they' Jesus is speaking about? They are those, in any time and place, who do not know 'the Father or me'. Everything turns on this in John; knowing it changes everything. There is no neutral ground. Not knowing the Father and Jesus is to be found resisting the message of the gospel.

We must also beware of assuming that 'they' means 'not me/us'. This continues to be a world in which appalling things are done in the name of God by people convinced that they are right. We can never underestimate the depths from which we need to be redeemed, but, in contrast to the pitiless certainties of those who believe that God calls them to violently exclude and murder, Jesus loves us. He knows well the support, comfort and encouragement his followers need in a world like this. Jesus' way of knowing is a fragile and vulnerable journey. It is easy to stumble. This faith is not fanaticism and its devotion never becomes dogmatism.

Jesus knows and understands all this and he speaks a word into our frailty: remember.

Prayer

I pray for those who will suffer today because they follow Jesus.

DAVID RUNCORN

John 16:4–6 (NRSV)

No questions?

'I did not say these things to you from the beginning, because I was with you. But now I am going to him who sent me; yet none of you asks me, "Where are you going?" But because I have said these things to you, sorrow has filled your hearts.'

There is nothing more frustrating for a teacher than getting no response to what they are saying. Is that what Jesus is feeling here? 'Have you not got any questions about what I am saying? No curiosity?' Asking is a continuing theme in this chapter.

Silence can be a sign of different things. It can be a lack of interest, of course, but it may be a lack of confidence. Grieving people may struggle for words and we know that Jesus' disciples at this point are full of grief. They are also struggling with thoughts and feelings outside their comprehension, as was so often the case when they were following and listening to Jesus.

We are also silent when we fear that our questions will expose our confusion and leave us embarrassed. In fact, nothing inhibits the quest to understand more than fearing our ignorance. Unless we take the risk, however, how will we come to the understanding that we most need?

In the Christian life, questions are the point at which we risk engagement, so they are more important than answers. Too often faith is assumed to be about submitting to God. Perhaps Jesus feels the same frustration with our prayers—or, rather, what we do not pray: 'You do not ask'! Faith is so much more than submission.

Jesus does not want passive, compliant followers. The disciples needed to ask more than Jesus needed to hear their questions. They needed drawing out. Now, there were times when Jesus reacted quite impatiently to questions that revealed their continued lack of understanding, but, in other encounters, he was hugely excited when people questioned and challenged what he was saying and drew him out further.

So, here Jesus seeks to provoke a response from his disciples. He seeks our questions, too, as they are a sign of faith—not a lack of it.

Reflection and prayer

May my questions become springboards for discovery.

David Runcorn

The Advocate will come

'I tell you the truth: it is to your advantage that I go away, for if I do not go away, the Advocate will not come to you; but if I go, I will send him to you. And when he comes, he will prove the world wrong about sin and righteousness and judgement: about sin, because they do not believe in me; about righteousness, because I am going to the Father and you will see me no longer; about judgement, because the ruler of this world has been condemned.'

Jesus insists his departure is good news. When he goes, 'the Advocate' will come. The word is another name for the Holy Spirit and is often translated as 'helper' or 'comforter', but it means so much more.

Imagine a cosmic courtroom. Two sides have come to present their case before the judge. On one side is 'the World' ('they' in verse 2), which is the ruling powers, authorities and controlling ideologies of our present age—those who rejected Jesus. We can imagine that side of the court packed with rows of the highest-paid lawyers and expert advisers. On the other side is a small, vulnerable group. Its members are poor, under-resourced and unimpressive. They cannot afford legal advice and lack both eloquence and learning. They are followers of Jesus. 'The World' holds them in contempt, but this group, says Jesus, is given 'the Advocate', who will take on, confront and totally demolish the claims of 'the World'.

Clearly that has not happened yet. That judgement is yet to be delivered, but this is revealed for our encouragement. We are to take comfort in the Holy Spirit, who is at work in the world now. For a while, there is little on the surface of life to suggest that this cosmic court will find in favour of such a fragile church on earth, but the Advocate is given, confronting 'the World' before the One whose judgement is true, challenging its ways, exposing its falsehoods, condemning its evils and vindicating the faithful by revealing the crucified one as Lord of all.

Prayer

Come, Holy Spirit, and declare what is true in the midst of a world of many falsehoods.

DAVID RUNCORN

What does he mean?

Then some of his disciples said to one another, 'What does he mean by saying to us, "A little while, and you will no longer see me, and again a little while, and you will see me"; and "Because I am going to the Father"?' They said, 'What does he mean by this "a little while"? We do not know what he is talking about.' Jesus knew that they wanted to ask him.

At three points in this chapter the focus is on the disciples and their questions about Jesus and what he is saying. We read the first on Monday. This was the time the disciples were silent in the face of what they could not understand, even though Jesus challenged them to question him. In today's passage, the disciples, as confused as ever, are asking questions, but they are murmuring their questions to each other. The word used here actually means something continuous—'They *kept on saying*, "What does he mean by this…?"'

Well, this is progress of a sort, but, if the first challenge was to ask questions at all, the second is surely to direct them to the one who can actually answer them! The picture here is of a group of people looking inwards, anxious, self-preoccupied, huddled together with their doubts and uncertainties.

All the while, Jesus seems to be standing nearby, quietly watching and waiting. One of the things that John stresses in these chapters is how completely Jesus knows his disciples. So we have, 'Jesus knew that they wanted to ask him' (v. 19). He understands, but it is never a knowledge that takes over. He never abuses his power over people: there is a gentleness and humility about the knowing of Jesus. In a world where 'knowledge is power' this is very good news, but we still have to believe it. Trust is a risk and we may have very good reasons for being reluctant to take the chance. Until we do, though, the questions will just keep on circling within us.

What if it is true that Jesus is saying, 'You only had to ask'?

Reflection

Are there questions you need to ask Jesus at this time?

DAVID RUNCORN

Labour pains

'Very truly, I tell you, you will weep and mourn, but the world will rejoice; you will have pain, but your pain will turn into joy. When a woman is in labour, she has pain, because her hour has come. But when her child is born, she no longer remembers the anguish because of the joy of having brought a human being into the world. So you have pain now; but I will see you again, and your hearts will rejoice, and no one will take your joy from you.'

Christian living in the world will be painful and costly, says Jesus. He wants his followers to be under no illusion about that, but he promises a final outcome that will eclipse whatever anguish has to be endured.

To illustrate, Jesus borrows from the experience of women in labour. His was a world long before modern medicine and pain relief. Childbirth was acutely hazardous—as it still is in many parts of the world—so this is not a comparison to be made lightly. It is a time of anguish, danger, vulnerability, wonder and joy. Jesus draws this parallel more than once when he is picturing the world descending into distress and violent turbulence. In Matthew's Gospel (24:8), he speaks of earthly upheavals as 'the birth pangs' of a new age.

We must understand this in the context of Jesus' own approaching death. Like a pregnant woman whose hour has come, he is in labour. This is his 'hour' (John 17:1). The trauma and anguish through which the world will be born to new life is upon him. He finds strength in contemplating what women endure in childbirth and the gift of life that results. For Jesus, listening to and learning from the experiences of women is particularly significant for the wisdom that sustains faith.

All this is for the strengthening of the faithful through the anguish of the present age. For Jesus, these painful 'contractions' foretell a joyful future. He invites us to imagine that amazing moment when, labour over, life emerges and the newborn is greeted, face to face.

Prayer

Lord, may our faith bring your life to birth within us.

DAVID RUNCORN

Ask!

'On that day you will ask nothing of me. Very truly, I tell you, if you ask anything of the Father in my name, he will give it to you. Until now you have not asked for anything in my name. Ask and you will receive, so that your joy may be complete.'

On what day? The reference is to the day Jesus was speaking of in the previous verses—that is, the day when, after the long anguish of labour, all comes together in a joyful birth. We will ask for nothing then because there will be nothing more to ask for! We will know, even as we have been fully known (1 Corinthians 13:12).

The contrast between that day and now is to be found in the asking. For Jesus, so much of our relationship with him and the Father is revealed in our willingness to and confidence in coming to him to ask. It is a measure of faith and understanding. Jesus offers his followers the privileged gift of knowing the Father, but this is not for spiritual name-dropping—'just mention my name'. Nor does the Father need incentives before giving us his attention. What this encouragement to ask reveals is the absolute unity of purpose, desire and longing between the Father and the Son. This asking flows from a recognition of who Jesus is, where he has come from and where he is going.

Actually the word 'ask' here should be translated as 'keep on asking'. The grammatical sense here is that it should be continuous. This is not because God has to be worn down before he will capitulate and give us what we want. The kind of asking Jesus urges here is better illustrated by the delightful but exhausting way children have of asking, out of a tireless curiosity about and fascination with life. Why? When? How? Where? It is an unselfconscious persistence that flows from a relationship of love and trust rather than the acquisitiveness of 'give me' or 'I want'.

This uninhibited, persistent pestering of the Father is matched by his desire to respond by giving it all to us. It is all joyfully mutual. So ask, says Jesus, and just go on asking.

Prayer

Father, may I pray with the delight and curiosity and trust of a child.

DAVID RUNCORN

Take courage

His disciples said, 'Yes, now you are speaking plainly, not in any figure of speech! Now we know that you know all things, and do not need to have anyone question you; by this we believe that you came from God.' Jesus answered them, 'Do you now believe? The hour is coming, indeed it has come, when you will be scattered, each one to his home, and you will leave me alone. Yet I am not alone because the Father is with me. I have said this to you, so that in me you may have peace. In the world you face persecution. But take courage; I have conquered the world!'

The chapter concludes precisely where it began. Jesus speaks again of 'the hour' that is coming (which is his crucifixion), warns of persecution and expresses concern that his disciples understand and are prepared for what is coming and do not fall away.

John uses a particular style of teaching here. We are more familiar with an approach that builds up to the main point at the end. In this chapter, though, Jesus teaches from both ends at once, building towards the key point in the middle. There we find the promise of the new day that is coming to birth, even now, through the anguished labour pains of Jesus' cross and the faithful suffering of his followers in this resistant age.

The chapter began with the disciples silent and uncomprehending, but now there has been a breakthrough. They finally understand! The way ahead is costly, but there is confidence, even excitement, in their words. Above all, they have grasped where Jesus has come from and, therefore, where he is going. For John, everything flows from that realisation.

Through it all, the longing of Jesus is the same—to help us understand and endure what faith may cost us and to live in hope that even the most anguished, painful contractions of this age are, in the overcoming death and resurrection of Jesus, signs of a new world coming to birth.

Reflection

Pause here and reflect on whether the themes of this chapter come to you as comfort or challenge.

DAVID RUNCORN

Sunday 22 March

JOHN 17:1–5 (NRSV)

Glory

After Jesus had spoken these words, he looked up to heaven and said, 'Father, the hour has come; glorify your Son so that the Son may glorify you, since you have given him authority over all people, to give eternal life to all whom you have given him. And this is eternal life, that they may know you, the only true God, and Jesus Christ whom you have sent. I glorified you on earth by finishing the work that you gave me to do. So now, Father, glorify me in your own presence with the glory that I had in your presence before the world existed.'

In chapter 16, Jesus was attending to his disciples on earth. Here the focus shifts, as he turns from earth and looks up to heaven. He is no longer speaking to his disciples, but is directly addressing the unseen Father, so we become privileged eavesdroppers on the prayer and conversation of the Son with the Father.

Notice how mutual is the relationship that reaches out to this world. The Son glorifies the Father; the Father glorifies the Son. Glorifying is a gift they give each other in loving submission. There is an utter unity of desire and purpose—nothing less than a world restored to the glory for which it was first made. This is all for our sake.

'The hour has come', says Jesus (John 17:1). All is complete. In John's Gospel 'the hour' is always the crucifixion. Very soon we will be reading of Jesus' arrest, torture and death. The crucifixion will be where his whole ministry on earth will find its complete expression and meaning. The cross, for John, is where the glory of God is revealed.

Does this sound strange? How can a crucifixion be glorious? Is the glory not in the triumph of the resurrection? This does not fit our preferred measures of success, power and victory. If, though, divine glory is revealed in a man who has been rejected and is dying on a cross, the story is changing. If glory is revealed there, in what is most lost, hopeless and Godforsaken, there is hope for all.

Prayer

Jesus, thank you for revealing your glory in what is lost and hopeless.

DAVID RUNCORN

Homecoming

'I have made your name known to those whom you gave me from the world. They were yours, and you gave them to me, and they have kept your word. Now they know that everything you have given me is from you; for the words that you gave to me I have given to them, and they have received them and know in truth that I came from you; and they have believed that you sent me. I am asking on their behalf; I am not asking on behalf of the world, but on behalf of those whom you gave me, because they are yours. All mine are yours, and yours are mine; and I have been glorified in them.'

Jesus continues to pray to the Father, although it sounds more like a debriefing at this point, with wording such as, 'I have made your name known' (v. 6). In the Bible, to reveal the name is to reveal the whole character and being of a person and to make them present. To know the name is to be committed to that person: 'those who know your name put their trust in you' (Psalm 9:10).

'They have kept your word' (John 17:6) seems a strange claim to make of such easily confused disciples, but the Father and Son know human frailty only too well. Perhaps this is not a claim of reliability so much as a way of expressing their commitment. How moving, too, that in their self-offering Jesus finds himself honoured: 'I have been glorified in them' (v. 10).

We must be wary of seeking to explain all this. Better to pause and acknowledge what a holy and intimate place we find ourselves in. After all, we are not accidental eavesdroppers on a conversation in a railway carriage. The reason we are hearing this prayer at all is because Jesus has brought us with him into the Father's presence. This is the heart of it. The Father does not have to be persuaded to accept us. Nor does he need us to be introduced to him. He knows us. We have always been his. Jesus has brought us home.

Reflection

I am in the presence of the Father, the Son and the Holy Spirit.
I am listening.

DAVID RUNCORN

Now

'And now I am no longer in the world, but they are in the world, and I am coming to you. Holy Father, protect them in your name that you have given me, so that they may be one, as we are one. While I was with them, I protected them in your name that you have given me. I guarded them, and not one of them was lost except the one destined to be lost, so that the scripture might be fulfilled.'

Two words express important themes in Jesus' prayer and they both occur in today's reading. 'Now' appears repeatedly throughout these chapters. John uses words that express time, to stress God's action in the world that is both present and imminent. 'Now' points us to Jesus' imminent betrayal and crucifixion.

The other word is 'protect'. Jesus is so evidently concerned for the welfare of his disciples. He knows very well the harrowing experiences they will be facing over the coming days. As he approaches his cross, it is a care he now hands over to the Father. His disciples will not be left alone. Nor are we.

Notice, too, the striking change of tense in Jesus' prayer at this point. He is speaking as if in some future place: 'I am no longer in the world' (v. 11). He also speaks of his earthly ministry as if looking back over something in the past, something achieved and now complete: 'while I was with them' (v. 12). It means that even the crucifixion is spoken of here as a past event.

This way of speaking is a dramatic device that John uses to highlight where history finds itself as the earthly ministry of Jesus approaches its terrible and glorious climax. God's future—that is still finally to be revealed—is nevertheless breaking in 'now'. Normal notions of time have collapsed. Our life in Christ now, through the Spirit, is a foretaste of what is to come. The eternal has entered history and opened it to the future. We are living in the overlap of the ages.

Prayer

Lord, help me to live today in the presence of the future.

DAVID RUNCORN

Joy

'But now I am coming to you, and I speak these things in the world so that they may have my joy made complete in themselves. I have given them your word, and the world has hated them because they do not belong to the world, just as I do not belong to the world. I am not asking you to take them out of the world, but I ask you to protect them from the evil one. They do not belong to the world, just as I do not belong to the world.'

'Our Christian joy drinks of the wellspring of [Jesus'] brimming heart'. This beautiful image comes from the first statement of faith by Pope Francis. The whole document, called *Evangelii Gaudeum* ('The Joy of the Gospel', I, 5) is simply full of joy.

Joy, says Pope Francis, is receiving, drinking in, the very life of Jesus, which is itself the life of God. It is pure gift. The focus, then, is not on enjoying the feeling but on who we are with. Joy is a side effect.

To know and be known in what Jesus calls 'the word' is to find our lives complete in the joy of God. This cannot be earned or deserved; it is pure gift. In his autobiography, C.S. Lewis famously described his moment of reluctant, intellectual submission to God. He was 'the most dejected and reluctant convert in all of England', but he called his book *Surprised by Joy* (1955, pp. 28–29).

Jesus speaks often of joy: 'I have said this to you so that... your joy may be complete' (15:11). It is a mark of confident, trusting prayer: 'Ask and you will receive, so that your joy may be complete' (16:24). This joy supported Jesus himself, even when facing suffering and death, as he, 'for the sake of the joy that was set before him endured the cross, disregarding its shame' (Hebrews 12:2).

There are echoes here of those declared blessed in the Sermon on the Mount (Matthew 5). We followers of Jesus are a strange community, living in the world but no longer belonging to it; hated for this, but full of joy.

Prayer

Let me drink from your brimming heart, Lord Jesus.

DAVID RUNCORN

Holy

'Sanctify them in the truth; your word is truth. As you have sent me into the world, so I have sent them into the world. And for their sakes I sanctify myself, so that they also may be sanctified in truth.'

'Sanctify' means 'to make holy', 'set apart' or 'consecrate' (*sanctus* is the Latin word for 'holy'). It is not to be reduced to the business of simply keeping thoughts pure and avoiding wrong actions. Important though these things are, the word means so much more. Who we are always comes before what we do or think. It is our whole being that Jesus is concerned for here.

So, when Jesus asks the Father to sanctify us, what is he praying for? We can easily miss how this request links to a recurring theme in Jesus' prayers for his followers—that we might be kept safe.

The ancient word 'sanctuary' comes from the same root as 'sanctify'. To give sanctuary is to bring endangered people into a place of shelter and protection. To be sanctified is to be brought under the holy protection of God. To be sanctified is also a call to worship. In traditional church buildings, the 'sanctuary' is the place where worship finds its deepest focus. In the glimpses of the worship of heaven that we find in the book of Revelation, the word 'holy' (*sanctus*) is repeated endlessly in awe and wonder as all heaven bows before the vision of God.

To 'consecrate' is another related word meaning to dedicate something or someone to a holy task. When we consecrate a building (such as a church) or people (for example, a bishop), we are setting them apart to be a particular expression of God's life and presence in the world. Jesus describes his whole earthly life among us as a personal consecration—a work of sanctification for us.

Only God can sanctify. That is why Jesus asks the Father to do this. It must be a gift. To be made holy is to be overshadowed and formed in the worship and life of God and to be found in his likeness and set apart for his service—like Jesus.

Prayer

Sanctify me, Lord.

David Runcorn

Welcome

'I ask not only on behalf of these, but also on behalf of those who will believe in me through their word, that they may all be one. As you, Father, are in me and I am in you, may they also be in us, so that the world may believe that you have sent me. The glory that you have given me I have given them, so that they may be one, as we are one, I in them and you in me, that they may become completely one, so that the world may know that you have sent me and have loved them even as you have loved me.'

While writing these notes I visited some friends who have just adopted a baby girl. Family, friends and neighbours were all invited to a welcome tea party for her. It was wonderfully moving. She sat on the floor, more interested in the wrapping paper than the presents, kicking with excitement and soaking in the love and joy that surrounded her. I looked around my friends' home and could see how it had been so lovingly prepared for her coming. No detail was missed. Everything spoke of delight in making a gift of their home and life to her and with her. That scene comes to mind as I read Jesus' words—'I in you', 'they in us', 'as we are one', 'loved even as you have loved me'. The tenderness, the generosity, the longing is almost overwhelming.

They in us, you in me, we are one… these almost sound like dance steps. In fact, when medieval theologians tried to express the love within the Trinity, they often pictured a round dance—the continual circling, the music, weaving in and out of one another, all gift and giving. The Trinity's longing, says Jesus, is to draw us into that dance. We are like hesitant watchers on the edge, a passing hand reaching out and pulling us in to a dance that contains everything: love, glory, knowing, unity. It has become the dance of our homecoming.

Prayer

Pull me into the dance of your eternal love, my God.

DAVID RUNCORN

Righted

> 'Righteous Father, the world does not know you, but I know you; and these know that you have sent me. I made your name known to them, and I will make it known, so that the love with which you have loved me may be in them, and I in them.'

At the conclusion of this prayer, an important word makes a single appearance. Jesus calls the Father 'righteous', a word often associated with judgement. After all, 'right' is the opposite of 'wrong', but it means much more than this.

Jesus points out again that this is a world that does not know the 'righteous Father'. If so, then something is not right at the very heart of the world. If the righteous Father is the source and centre of existence, there can be no more fundamental disordering than this. 'Righteous' here can mean 'right ordering', of things being in their proper place. The word also suggests a work of rehabilitation. A world that does not know God rightly cannot know itself rightly either. It will be completely off balance—like a boat foundering and in danger of capsizing. We need righting.

What we do and do not know has been a recurring central theme in these chapters. For John, knowing who Jesus is, where he came from and where he is going is the knowledge that unlocks everything. In returning to the Father, Jesus goes to the one in whom it is all 'right'. The way in which the world will be righted and rehabilitated to the Father is through the only one who knows the Father—Jesus. He 'right-eouses' us (we need a verb here, which the English language does not have!) When we live in the truth of this, our lives are 'righted' and all things are restored to their true places.

Once again, it is Jesus' firm confidence and foresight that we hear: 'I know', 'I made… known', 'I will make it known' (vv. 25–26). Prayer is what Jesus does in us, for us. All this is his gift and we can trust him with our lives.

Prayer

Righteous Father, may my life find its true balance and meaning in you.

David Runcorn

Pilgrims to the cross

The church's year has now come round to Holy Week and Easter, the climax of the long weeks of Lent. Consumer societies focus relentlessly on celebrating Christmas, with the countdown to the shopping frenzy seeming to begin earlier each time, but, without Holy Week and Easter, Christmas is meaningless. A miraculous child was born, true, but his destiny was only fulfilled in his death and resurrection, firstfruits of a redeemed creation. Without the death and without the resurrection, we would have, at best, no more than ancient stories of an exemplary man who lived centuries ago, an inspiring character but no heaven-sent Saviour.

Our faith should find its foundation and fruition in this season, yet, too often, I myself have arrived at Good Friday unfocused, overly busy and ill prepared for the deep reflection that should characterise the days to follow.

In some ways it can be easier to immerse ourselves in the wonder of Christmas. After all, the birth of every baby feels miraculous. As a midwife once commented to me, 'I still find it amazing. One minute there are, say, four people in the room. The next, there is a new human being, taking his or her first breaths.'

Death is something that we find harder to deal with. In the case of Jesus' crucifixion, it is death as horrific public execution. It is so tempting to avert our gaze, press forward to the relief of Easter morning, overlooking the fact that, for Jesus' family and followers, this death was a catastrophe, something they had refused to countenance. Perhaps they were hoping that his sombre hints and warnings of the previous weeks were not to be taken at face value, thinking, 'How can this newly revealed Messiah, God's Anointed One, die? And die like that?'

I invite you, then, to accompany me over the next couple of weeks, joining Christian believers around the world who will follow the way of Jesus to the cross and beyond to the astonishing empty tomb. I invite you to be a pilgrim with me, journeying in search of new understanding of the ways of our world and our God, fresh insights into the meaning and significance of what it means to live as Jesus' followers today.

Naomi Starkey

Save us!

[The disciples] brought the colt to Jesus and threw their cloaks on it; and he sat on it. Many people spread their cloaks on the road, and others spread leafy branches that they had cut in the fields. Then those who went ahead and those who followed were shouting, 'Hosanna! Blessed is the one who comes in the name of the Lord!'... Then he entered Jerusalem and went into the temple; and when he had looked around at everything, as it was already late, he went out to Bethany with the twelve.

The crowds press around us, pilgrims like ourselves, coming to Jerusalem for the great Passover feast. The journey may have been long and hard for many, but now the city gates are in sight and the celebratory psalm-singing begins. The noise, the jostling, the excitement grow by the moment and here is Jesus, riding an unbroken colt through the throng, an entrance carefully prepared by his followers, right down to the road carpeted in coats and branches.

It is extraordinary that the colt is not spooked by the chaos: there seem to be no fears of this rider taking an ignominious tumble. The one who calmed the wind and waves can calm a nervous animal, too. This must surely be the moment when the Messiah's public reign begins. After the years of itinerant preaching, at last all eyes will look on him with wonder and worship.

Then, however, disappointingly, he seems to behave like every other pilgrim. A quick look at the city's sights, including the all-important visit to the temple, in so many ways the centrepoint of the city, followed by what feels like a retreat to Bethany. Of course, some of his closest friends live there—Mary, Martha and Lazarus—and it is no doubt a pleasant place to stay instead of the busy streets of Jerusalem, but time is pressing for the Messiah to be revealed to the world. Surely this is no time for social calls?

Reflection

Jesus lived and breathed the purposes of God, but they did not drive out his human need for rest, recreation and companionship. Do we permit ourselves to acknowledge such needs?

NAOMI STARKEY

Troublemaker

Then they came to Jerusalem. And he entered the temple and began to drive out those who were selling and those who were buying in the temple, and he overturned the tables of the money-changers and the seats of those who sold doves; and he would not allow anyone to carry anything through the temple. He was teaching and saying, 'Is it not written, "My house shall be called a house of prayer for all the nations"? But you have made it a den of robbers.'

Why would Jesus never take the predictable path? Return to Jerusalem—good; return to the temple—appropriate. But now he sets about over-turning the stalls providing the necessary items for the system of sacrifices. He is outrageous enough to accuse respectable traders of being robbers. He goes so far as to stop anyone carrying anything through the temple. This is, by any reckoning, unnecessarily antagonistic.

This is a familiar story and can lose the shocking impact it would have had at the time. Imagine this disruptive energy being unleashed in a cathedral today—audio guides being knocked off the counter, Bibles grabbed from the gift shop shelves and handed to gawping visitors and the ticket barrier (if there is one) falling to a deftly wielded crowbar. 'This is a place for praying,' shouts the vandalising (and, frankly, terrifying) figure. 'Who is praying here? Who instead is just doing their shopping or having a history lesson? You and you and you—get out! GET OUT!!'

The next verses tell us that the chief priests and scribes reacted extremely badly to this temple incident, putting Jesus on their hit list. We cannot assume that our own response would have been so different, especially if we were in some way guardians of the place under attack.

Seeing such up-ending of expectations should remind us that, while Jesus is friend, good shepherd and healer, he is also God incarnate, filled with the power that tamed chaos and brought creation to birth. We should not presume to second guess what he would or would not approve of, but humbly listen for the prompting of his Spirit.

Reflection

If Jesus visited our own place of worship, what might he challenge or even overturn?

NAOMI STARKEY

Absolutely everything

He sat down opposite the treasury, and watched the crowd putting money into the treasury. Many rich people put in large sums. A poor widow came and put in two small copper coins, which are worth a penny. Then he called his disciples and said to them, 'Truly I tell you, this poor widow has put in more than all those who are contributing to the treasury. For all of them have contributed out of their abundance; but she out of her poverty has put in everything she had, all she had to live on.'

If yesterday's reading showed us a discomfiting, even threatening Jesus, today we read of an encounter that is so moving in the tender compassion he showed towards one whose status was among the lowliest in society at that time. In recognising the true worth of the widow's offering, Jesus exemplifies the revolution that had been anticipated in his own mother's song, Mary's Magnificat (Luke 1:46–55), with the needy honoured and the rich sent away empty in a divine up-ending of the usual ways of the world.

Yet, we should not make the mistake of patronising this woman: 'Bless her, poor thing! What a shame for someone to be so destitute.' Such pity sees only poverty and apparent weakness when, in truth, this woman (defined according to the conventions of the time only by her marital status or, rather, lack of it) shows immense courage and cast-iron faith. Let us suppose she made her decision after due and prayerful consideration: even so, which of us would consider the option of emptying our savings account and giving it all in obedience to what we believe are God's purposes?

The consoling truth at the heart of this story is this: God notices our sacrifices. He is not distracted by the loudest voice, the flashiest credit card, the most senior rank. This woman came to the temple, humbly and unheralded, and gave everything. Jesus saw what she had done and drew others' attention to her actions. Perhaps, who knows, some of those he told about her were moved to offer her help.

Reflection

Do we really believe and trust in God's provision for us?

Naomi Starkey

In the leper's house

While he was at Bethany in the house of Simon the leper, as he sat at the table, a woman came with an alabaster jar of very costly ointment of nard, and she broke open the jar and poured the ointment on his head. But some were there who said to one another in anger, 'Why was the ointment wasted in this way? For this ointment could have been sold for more than three hundred denarii, and the money given to the poor.' And they scolded her. But Jesus said, 'Let her alone; why do you trouble her? She has performed a good service for me.'

This beautiful story involves a wildly extravagant act. The precious ointment was worth nearly a year's wage. A rough estimate might set the figure at around £9000. That was the value of what was poured out on Jesus' head, yet his reaction, once again, subverts normal expectations. Sitting among those gathered in that room, we would have been overwhelmed by the fragrance of the anointing. Then we would remember the turmoil in the temple courts and Jesus' praise for the generous widow and we would probably shake our heads, baffled by this rabbi's strange value system. Whenever we think we have worked it out, everything shifts again. We love him, we follow him, but he never makes the rules clear enough. He is always one step ahead of us.

The narrative here focuses on Jesus and the woman, but we should also note the setting—the house of Simon the leper. What the Bible describes as 'leprosy' may or may not have been the mildly infectious condition also known as Hansen's disease, effective treatment for which was not developed until the 1940s. Whatever the precise diagnosis, anybody suffering from such a disease in Jesus'time (as for centuries before and after) was feared and shunned, permanently judged 'unclean'.

How does Jesus respond to Simon's situation? He accepts a dinner invitation. He relaxes, eats, drinks, socialises with the outcast and, in so doing, he challenges us to do likewise.

Reflection

Who are the 'outcasts' in your community? What can you and your church do to connect with them?

NAOMI STARKEY

Deserted

When they had sung the hymn, they went out to the Mount of Olives. And Jesus said to them, 'You will all become deserters; for it is written, "I will strike the shepherd, and the sheep will be scattered." But after I am raised up, I will go before you to Galilee.' Peter said to him, 'Even though all become deserters, I will not.' Jesus said to him, 'Truly I tell you, this day, this very night, before the cock crows twice, you will deny me three times.' But he said vehemently, 'Even though I must die with you, I will not deny you.' And all of them said the same.

When we retell the story of Gethsemane, it is tempting to focus on the betrayal by Judas, but Jesus' words here are uncompromising: 'You will all become deserters' (v. 27). Peter is included, too, and it can be tempting to speak disparagingly of the big fisherman, so outspoken yet so cowardly in the end. It seems unthinkable that we, too, might have abandoned Jesus, but we should be careful before confidently claiming that we would have done better had we been there that night.

The full extent of the desertion is clear if we read today's passage in context. In verse 18, Jesus confronts his followers with the fact that one of them will betray him, which makes them 'distressed' (v. 19). In the verses following today's passage, Jesus withdraws with his three closest friends—Peter, James and John—who then fall asleep instead of comforting him as he agonises in prayer. Then comes the appalling conclusion: 'All of them deserted him and fled' (v. 50) as the religious authorities and a heated crowd came to arrest him. Jesus has to face his trial alone, too, and the knowledge that he had foreseen this circumstance is unlikely to have been consoling.

In many churches, the altar is stripped after the Maundy Thursday Eucharist (which may include a foot-washing ceremony) and the consecrated Communion wafers are taken to a side chapel where people gather in silent meditation, remembering Jesus' lonely vigil in Gethsemane. It is a time to watch, wait and pray.

Reflection

'Could you not keep awake one hour?' (Mark 14:37).

NAOMI STARKEY

Dying alone

At three o' clock Jesus cried out with a loud voice, '*Eloi, Eloi, lema sabachthani*?' which means 'My God, my God, why have you forsaken me?' When some of the bystanders heard it, they said, 'Listen, he is calling for Elijah.' And someone ran, filled a sponge with sour wine, put it on a stick, and gave it to him to drink, saying, 'Wait, let us see whether Elijah will come to take him down.' Then Jesus gave a loud cry and breathed his last. And the curtain of the temple was torn in two, from top to bottom.

There has been darkness, three long hours of it, and, according to Mark (v. 25), Jesus had already been hanging on the cross for three hours before that strange darkness fell. How long those hours will have seemed for the women, those who loved and provided for Jesus on his travels and were 'looking on from a distance' at his dying agony (v. 40).

The cross has become such an icon of redemption that it may be startling to realise it was not adopted as such until the fifth century. Jesus was executed by a grotesque method, one designed for maximum pain and humiliation. What Mark records here sounds like misunderstanding and mockery, right to the end, as Jesus cries out the opening words of Psalm 22, words that exactly capture his physical, emotional and spiritual state. The tremendous drama of the temple curtain tearing in two takes place offstage, so that all we see here, at the place of the skull, is blood and death. Even the centurion's acclamation is in the past tense: 'this man was God's Son' (v. 39).

Today, churches hold services commemorating Christ's suffering and death. They may end in silence, with the priest walking out without giving a final blessing, switching off the lights to symbolise the extinguishing of Jesus' earthly life. The congregation is left, as the first followers were, in the shadows.

Reflection

When something comes to an end, we may carry on seeking signs of life, of hope, but sometimes we have to accept that we must simply grieve for what has gone.

NAOMI STARKEY

A brave man

When evening had come, and since it was the day of Preparation, that is, the day before the sabbath, Joseph of Arimathea, a respected member of the council, who was also himself waiting expectantly for the kingdom of God, went boldly to Pilate and asked for the body of Jesus... Then Joseph bought a linen cloth, and taking down the body, wrapped it in the linen cloth, and laid it in a tomb that had been hewn out of the rock. He then rolled a stone against the door of the tomb. Mary Magdalene and Mary the mother of Joses saw where the body was laid.

The Jewish sabbath begins at sundown the evening before, which, as the passage states, would have been one of the reasons Joseph went to Pilate so soon after Jesus' death to request the body for burial. That and, let us surmise, the desire to remove the dead Messiah and lay him to rest, hidden from the shame and ridicule of public gaze. At least in death Jesus receives some honour—laid in a rich man's tomb, cut from the rock. Perhaps the hurry to finish all work before sundown (as the Law decreed) was why the women had to return the next morning, bringing the appropriate spices for anointing a corpse. 'Joses' in the passage, by the way, is a Greek form of Joseph, not a misprint for Jesus. Verse 40 identifies him as a brother of 'James the younger', who may or may not have been one of the twelve disciples.

Publicly identifying with an executed rebel (from the Romans' perspective) and blasphemer (as the Jewish authorities saw Jesus) would have demanded enormous courage from Joseph because the repercussions for such actions could have been severe and wide-ranging. As recently as 1983, when Carmen Bugan was barely in her teens, her father staged a protest against the communist regime in Romania. Not only was he arrested and imprisoned but also the whole family suffered bitterly, as she tells in her powerful memoir *Burying the Typewriter* (Picador, 2013).

Reflection

Today, Holy Saturday, is a day for quiet reflection after the anguish of Good Friday. Then, at dusk, the Easter Vigil can begin, preparing us for that most astonishing of reversals tomorrow.

NAOMI STARKEY

MARK 16:1–6 (NRSV, ABRIDGED)

He is not here

When the sabbath was over, Mary Magdalene, and Mary the mother of James, and Salome bought spices, so that they might go and anoint him… They had been saying to one another, 'Who will roll away the stone for us from the entrance to the tomb?' When they looked up, they saw that the stone… had already been rolled back. As they entered the tomb, they saw a young man, dressed in a white robe, sitting on the right side; and they were alarmed. But he said to them, 'Do not be alarmed; you are looking for Jesus of Nazareth, who was crucified. He has been raised; he is not here.'

And so the women come 'very early' (v. 2) to complete the burial rites, imagining, as they make their way to the tomb, the scene awaiting them. The body will no longer be stiffened by rigor mortis, making their work of anointing easier, but that final act of love appears blocked by an immovable obstacle. If that obstacle is too heavy for two women working together, what chance for a terribly wounded young man, revived from his coma by the coolness of the rock chamber, trying to push from inside? Not that Jesus' followers are in any doubt that he is dead for surely if there had been the tiniest sign of life left in him, they would not have sealed him in that tomb.

In his rising, as in his living and dying, Jesus confounds expectations once again. If we did not know the story so well, if we were hearing it for the first time, we might find the details verging on the hilarious, inducing incredulous laughter along with tears of wonder. That great stone has already been rolled back; inside the tomb is no body but a mysterious young man, very much alive; the women's natural alarm is dismissed because their friend's body has somehow disappeared. This, though, is no story of a grave robbery. The one who was indisputably dead is now alive again.

Reflection

The joy of Easter does not have to be a solemn joy; it can be a festive roar of delight. The impossible has happened—death has been defeated.

NAOMI STARKEY

What happened next

[The young man said] 'But go, tell his disciples and Peter that he is going ahead of you to Galilee; there you will see him, just as he told you.' So [the women] went out and fled from the tomb, for terror and amazement had seized them; and they said nothing to anyone, for they were afraid. And all that had been commanded them they told briefly to those around Peter. And afterwards Jesus himself sent out through them, from east to west, the sacred and imperishable proclamation of eternal salvation.'

We now reach one of the imponderables of Mark's Gospel—the ending. Nowadays, most scholars agree that the original text ended abruptly in the middle of verse 8, with the words translated as 'for they were afraid'. Today, we have the first of two alternative conclusions to the dramatic events of Easter Day, which tidy up the story to indicate that the women did do what the heavenly messenger told them to do, albeit 'briefly'. Then there is a kind of snapshot of Jesus' final commission to his followers, as told at greater length at the end of Matthew's Gospel.

The abruptness of the original ending, though, fits the abrupt narrative nature of Mark, with its vivid and rapidly changing scenes and dramatic tension. The women's reaction underlines the stupendous nature of the Easter event. 'He is dead'; 'No, he isn't'; 'So where is he?', 'Waiting for you back in Galilee, like he promised.' It is hardly surprising that the women flee in 'terror and amazement' (v. 8): the whole situation is more than the mind can take in. As before, if we try to imagine hearing it all for the first time, the story is actually quite funny. The women do not fall to their knees and honour the heavenly messenger. Instead, they run away and say nothing.

Even if the expanded ending is textually dubious, history shows that the women must have told at least one person. The first witnesses to the staggeringly good news of the resurrection did not stay silent. Joy and faith eventually won out over their fear and confusion.

Reflection

Where is Jesus? Gone ahead of us, as he always does,
waiting for us to follow.

Naomi Starkey

What else happened next

Now after he rose early on the first day of the week, he appeared first to Mary Magdalene, from whom he had cast out seven demons. She went out and told those who had been with him, while they were mourning and weeping. But when they heard that he was alive and had been seen by her, they would not believe it. After this he appeared in another form to two of them, as they were walking into the country. And they went back and told the rest, but they did not believe them.

For the next three days, we will read passages from the second alternative conclusion to Mark's Gospel (see yesterday's notes for more on the alternative endings). Based on a high incidence of vocabulary not found elsewhere in Mark's Gospel, plus strong parallels with post-resurrection accounts in Matthew, Luke and John, as well as Acts, scholars now surmise that this section was not part of the original text.

It is interesting, though, to read these verses for the somewhat different light they shed on those early days of Easter. In telling that story, we may tend (naturally enough) to conflate the four Gospels and forget how each writer shaped the material to bring out particular truths and emphases. We can move, Hollywood-style, from John's radiant dawn meeting between Jesus and Mary Magdalene in the garden to Luke's vivid Emmaus road scene to Matthew's hilltop farewell tableau and forget to read each account on its own terms, noting what is included and omitted.

Even if the status of these final verses is doubtful, they are still in tune with Mark's overall emphasis on exploring how people respond to Jesus, both the Saviour himself and his teaching. Here we have the radiant John scene and the vivid Luke scene almost deflated by the disbelief of those hearing the reports of what had happened. The good news is treated as a tall tale, a wish-fulfilment fantasy brought on by the stress of bereavement. The saying goes that 'if something is too good to be true, it usually is'. But not where the kingdom of heaven is concerned.

Reflection
How open are we to being astonished by God?

NAOMI STARKEY

Rebuked

Later he appeared to the eleven themselves as they were sitting at the table; and he upbraided them for their lack of faith and stubbornness, because they had not believed those who saw him after he had risen. And he said to them 'Go into all the world and proclaim the good news to the whole creation. The one who believes and is baptised will be saved; but the one who does not believe will be condemned.'

The abrupt, bubble-puncturing tone of this alternative ending continues. John's Gospel presents us with Jesus bestowing peace and the Holy Spirit on his frightened friends (20:19–22), reassuring the doubter (vv. 27–29), and that wonderful beach breakfast episode (21:1–23). Luke provides equal measures of reassurance and explanation (24:36–49). Here, Jesus sounds almost brusque, a tone of voice found in other passages in Mark, such as the cursing of the fig tree (11:12–14), fruitless simply because it was not the season for figs.

Such brusqueness is, surely, what we also hear in the voice of God, confronted yet again by the stubborn rebellion of his people, even as they wandered in the wilderness after the exodus, dependent on heavenly food and heavenly guidance. We hear it in the anger of the prophets, as their divinely inspired warnings fall unheeded. We see it across the Gospels, as Jesus turns on the religious leaders who are failing in their duty of care for the people. God has, since the very beginning, loved humanity, longed for them to listen and lamented their turning away.

We may find the final words in today's passage very uncomfortable. Indeed, 'condemned' sounds horrifyingly harsh, but if the Son of God brings salvation, then whoever does not accept the Son of God cannot receive that salvation. This is a logical consequence, not punishment. What is not spelled out here, though, is the timescale for such condemnation—and we have an infinite God, with infinite love and infinite patience. That is the context for such uncomfortable words.

Reflection

Jesus says, too, that they are to preach 'to the whole creation'. What might be good news for the non-human parts of creation?

NAOMI STARKEY

Wonder-working

[Jesus said] 'And these signs will accompany those who believe: by using my name they will cast out demons; they will speak in new tongues; they will pick up snakes in their hands, and if they drink any deadly thing, it will not hurt them; they will lay their hands on the sick, and they will recover.' So then the Lord Jesus, after he had spoken to them, was taken up into heaven and sat down at the right hand of God. And they went out and proclaimed the good news everywhere, while the Lord worked with them and confirmed the message by the signs that accompanied it.

Many of the 'signs' listed here by Jesus are found in the book of Acts, including Paul's encounter with a poisonous snake after his shipwreck (28:3–5). Commentators are at pains to point out that Jesus is not condoning such behaviour—as if downing a pint of poison is a valid way of demonstrating God's power and protection. Having said that, a relatively small number of Pentecostal-style churches in the USA claim inspiration from these verses to include snake-handling and drinking strychnine in their worship services, with occasionally (and unsurprisingly) fatal results.

Whatever our preferred style of worship, we should seek signs of God at work in our community, in the wider world and in our own lives. We would be equally mistaken to deny that God can act miraculously here and now as to base our faith entirely on signs of the more spectacular kind. Of course, the eternal, omnipotent Lord of space and time can heal, for example, but we should never assume that healing is somehow less holy because it comes about through modern medical expertise, rather than being drug-free and instantaneous.

The point is not the sign in itself, however headline-grabbing it might be, but the faith generated by a combination of gospel message shared and heavenly grace received.

Reflection

Jesus' followers are sent out into a hostile world, with the reminder that the power of God's kingdom surrounds and sustains them as they go—as we are still sent and as we are still surrounded and sustained.

Naomi Starkey

Hospitality

Hospitality can come in all shapes and sizes and, over the next nine days, the Bible passages and our reflections on them will aim to scratch the surface of some of the varied forms it may take. In the first passage, from Romans (echoed in Hebrews), Paul's heartfelt plea is that we 'let love be genuine' and that we should bring the quality of this authentic love to all our relationships. The second passage, from Genesis 18, considers Abraham's welcome to three mysterious strangers, taking our reflection on the theme of hospitality further and deeper.

The well-known incident in which Jesus visits the home of Mary and Martha (Luke 10:38–42) challenges our often-held view that good hospitality is all about the outward preparations. Monday's reading takes this idea further as we explore Jesus' ultimate form of hospitality— the giving of his life for the life of the world. In their different ways, the next two passages bring the challenge to be hospitable very close to home. The widow of Zarephath (1 Kings 17:10–16) is asked for food by Elijah at a time when she and her son are at the point of starvation. Judas' acceptance of bread at Jesus' table and his subsequent betrayal offer a classic example of hospitality abused.

In a passage from Luke 7, Jesus rebukes his host Simon the Pharisee for his totally inadequate hospitality, comparing it unfavourably with the loving welcome offered to him by a woman of the city who was a 'sinner'. In the reading from Luke 14, Jesus stresses that there is no room, in genuine hospitality, for mixed motives. There is no place for self-interest of any kind; we should welcome others with warm acceptance and no expectation of repayment or hope of any possible future advantage to ourselves.

Our sequence of readings is brought to a close with a passage from Revelation 7. As those who have 'washed their robes… in the blood of the Lamb' (v. 14) gather around the throne, the writer looks forward to that time at the completion of all things when the hunger and thirst of all people will be satisfied, when the Lamb will be their shepherd and all suffering will be banished from God's kingdom of love, justice and peace.

Barbara Mosse

Welcoming friend and stranger

Let love be genuine; hate what is evil, hold fast to what is good; love one another with a mutual affection; outdo one another in showing honour. Do not lag in zeal, be ardent in spirit, serve the Lord. Rejoice in hope, be patient in suffering, persevere in prayer. Contribute to the needs of the saints; extend hospitality to strangers... Let brotherly love continue. Be not forgetful to entertain strangers, for thereby some have entertained angels unawares.

In these verses from the letter to the Romans, echoed by the author of Hebrews, Paul appears to set the bar dauntingly high. Love is to be genuine, there should be mutual affection and Christians are to outdo each other in showing honour. So, it may be useful to note what comes immediately before this passage, which is a stern warning from Paul about the dangers of overcompetitiveness, some teaching about the body of Christ and the need for each individual member of that body to regard all the others as being equal to themselves.

The needs of the saints and the injunction to be hospitable to strangers may seem almost an afterthought, but, clearly, a community unable to express love and mutual acceptance among its own members is unlikely to be able to offer warm and generous hospitality to outsiders.

In the sixth-century *Rule of Benedict* (RB), the importance of hospitality is similarly emphasised. We sometimes fear the demands that openness to the needs of others may lay upon us. Indeed, such commitment is often costly in both time and energy, but those following Benedict's way of life today make clear that it is often possible to offer hospitality in the most fleeting of moments: 'We often encounter opportunities to make room in our schedules, in ourselves, for another person. Yet the moment can come and go quickly. Consciously be aware when someone needs a moment of kindness, a little attention, a gracious gesture. Do this both at home and at work' (Pratt and Homan, *Benedict's Way*, p. 69).

Reflection

In the reception of the poor and of pilgrims the greatest care and solicitude should be shown, because it is especially in them that Christ is received.

Rule of Benedict, Chapter 53

BARBARA MOSSE

Entertaining angels unawares

The Lord appeared to Abraham by the oaks of Mamre, as he sat at the entrance of his tent in the heat of the day. He looked up and saw three men standing near him. When he saw them, he ran from the tent entrance to meet them, and bowed down to the ground. He said, 'My lord, if I find favour with you, do not pass by your serv-ant. Let a little water be brought, and wash your feet, and rest yourselves under the tree. Let me bring a little bread, that you may refresh yourselves, and after that you may pass on—since you have come to your servant.' So they said, 'Do as you have said.'

When the author of yesterday's passage from the letter to the Hebrews wrote that those offering hospitality to strangers may well be 'entertain-ing angels unawares', it could be that he had this incident from Genesis in his mind.

In today's passage, we are given information not revealed to Abra-ham until much later in the narrative—that these visitors are not ordi-nary travellers, but heavenly beings. Abraham's lavish hospitality has several characteristics and follows a pattern typical in the Middle East during this period. It involved seeing, running to meet, honouring, inviting, preparing food and serving. The low bow would be made to every visitor (not just the 'important' ones!)

In today's world, the many troubling varieties of all-too-real 'stranger danger'—whether online or in person—make this form of hospitality especially challenging. Our dilemma has no easy answer, but it may be helpful to remember that biblical hospitality involves openness not only to other people but also, pre-eminently, to God. Jesus would later stress the need for discernment in our dealings with others, when he advised his disciples to be 'wise as serpents and innocent as doves' (Matthew 10:16). We are not expected to act either naively or without prayer.

Reflection

Living is simple when the threshold is smooth enough for the innocent to cross and enter our lives and strong enough to bar the beguilers. God rightly frames the door to our souls and our lives as promised…

Martin Marty and Micah Marty, *When True Simplicity is Gained*, p. 32

Barbara Mosse

117

A welcoming heart

Now as they went on their way, he entered a certain village, where a woman named Martha welcomed [Jesus] into her home. She had a sister named Mary, who sat at the Lord's feet and listened to what he was saying. But Martha was distracted by her many tasks; so she came to him and asked, 'Lord, do you not care that my sister has left me to do all the work by myself? Tell her then to help me.' But the Lord answered her, 'Martha, Martha, you are worried and distracted by many things; there is need of only one thing. Mary has chosen the better part, which will not be taken away from her.'

Most traditional interpretations of this passage have tended to compare the active life of the Christian (Martha) with the contemplative life (Mary), to the considerable disadvantage of the former. This view actually begs as many questions as it claims to answer. Martha has welcomed Jesus into her home, so is Jesus' response to her complaint a slap in the face? Mary's sitting and listening to Jesus is claimed to be 'the better part', so where, then, does this leave those whose work on behalf of others is necessarily 'active'?

It is possible, though, to read this incident in other ways. Jesus' words to Martha can be interpreted not as a rude rejection of her generous hospitality but, rather, as a challenge to a lack of single-heartedness in her work. The work she was doing was, after all, vital—without it there would have been no refreshments for their weary visitor. Instead of carrying out her self-chosen tasks with energy and commitment, however, Martha is resentful that Mary has chosen to listen to Jesus rather than join her in her fretful distraction. The 'better part' that Jesus is commending is Mary's single-mindedness; had Martha been similarly focused, Mary's stillness would not have worried her and there would have been no need for Jesus' rebuke.

Reflection

Do you have a tendency to suspect that the grass is always greener elsewhere? As you engage with today's tasks, try to bring to each activity a sense of single-hearted commitment that comes from the very centre of your being.

Barbara Mosse

Ultimate hospitality

Jesus said to them, 'Very truly, I tell you, it was not Moses who gave you the bread from heaven, but it is my Father who gives you the true bread from heaven. For the bread of God is that which comes down from heaven and gives life to the world.' They said to him, 'Sir, give us this bread always.' Jesus said to them, 'I am the bread of life. Whoever comes to me will never be hungry, and whoever believes in me will never be thirsty.'

One of the most famous and well-loved poems by the 17th-century priest-poet George Herbert, 'Love III', begins, 'Love bade me welcome; yet my soul drew back, guilty of dust and sin.' The writer has a powerful sense of himself as a sinner who is invited by God—Love—to sit down at God's table and be served by him. The sinner's fears and excuses are eventually overcome by Love's gentle but insistent persuasion and, in humble gratitude, he accepts the hospitality of God and allows himself to be fed.

The poem has some resonance with today's passage from John's Gospel. Jesus is reminding the people that it was not Moses who fed their ancestors manna in the wilderness; it was their heavenly Father, who continues to give life to the world through his Son, Jesus ('I am the bread of life', v. 35).

This passage challenges us to ask ourselves in what places we look for our nourishment. We may not take refuge in the sex, drugs and alcohol addictions that are the resort of so many in their desperate attempts to fill the emptiness within, but we may be vulnerable to other, more subtle temptations. Are we, for instance, slaves to television? Do we eat more than we need? Jesus is the ultimate host, but are we so involved in 'good works' or church activities—a little like Martha, perhaps (see yesterday's notes)—that we have no time left to simply 'be' with Jesus or respond to his gracious invitation to come to him?

Reflection

'Every generous act of giving, with every perfect gift, is from above, coming down from the Father of lights, with whom there is no variation or shadow'
(James 1:17).

BARBARA MOSSE

An exercise in trust

When [Elijah] came to [Zarephath], a widow was there gathering sticks; he called to her and said, 'Bring me a little water in a vessel, so that I may drink... [and] a morsel of bread in your hand.' But she said, 'As the Lord your God lives, I have nothing baked, only a handful of meal in a jar, and a little oil in a jug; I am now gathering a couple of sticks, so that I may go home and prepare it for myself and my son, that we may eat it, and die.' Elijah said to her, 'Do not be afraid; go and do as you have said; but first make me a little cake of it and bring it to me... For thus says the Lord the God of Israel: The jar of meal will not be emptied and the jug of oil will not fail.'

Zarephath, normally a prosperous city, was struggling because of a severe drought. In such circumstances, the requirement to offer hospitality would be testing for anyone, but for a widow, such a demand would be particularly challenging. In scripture, widows are frequently paired with orphans as among the poorest and most destitute in society (Deuteronomy 16:11; Isaiah 9:17; James 1:27). When Elijah asks the woman for food, following God's command to him (1 Kings 17:8–9), the desperate plight of her and her son is revealed. The oath she uses to preface her reply echoes Elijah's own at the beginning of the chapter (vv. 1, 12) and her test of trust has added severity as she is a Phoenician and does not share Elijah's faith ('As the Lord your God lives').

Would we be capable of offering open-hearted hospitality to someone who did not share our faith or worldview and at a time when our own resources were stretched beyond their limit?

Reflection

'[Jesus] sat down opposite the treasury... A poor widow came and put in two small copper coins. Then he called his disciples and said to them, "Truly I tell you, this poor widow has put in more than all those who are contributing to the treasury... she out of her poverty has put in everything she had, all she had to live on"' (Mark 12:41–44).

BARBARA MOSSE

Hospitality abused

Jesus was troubled in spirit, and declared, 'Very truly, I tell you, one of you will betray me.' The disciples looked at one another, uncertain of whom he was speaking. One of his disciples—the one whom Jesus loved—was reclining next to him; Simon Peter therefore motioned to him to ask Jesus of whom he was speaking. So... he asked him, 'Lord, who is it?' Jesus answered, 'It is the one to whom I give this piece of bread when I have dipped it in the dish.' So when he had dipped the piece of bread, he gave it to Judas son of Simon Iscariot... After receiving the piece of bread, he immediately went out. And it was night.

The scene here is one of great intimacy. Jesus is hosting a final Passover supper for his closest friends, but there is a spectre at the feast. Jesus is 'troubled in spirit' (v. 21) by his highly tuned discernment of Judas' intentions, but at no point does he reject Judas because of this. Jesus personally dips the bread in the bowl and hands it to Judas. Judas accepts it and then immediately leaves the group, with the Gospel writer's added comment, 'It was night' (v. 30), emphasising the 'darkness' of his action.

Jesus' stance here is consistent with that which he takes elsewhere. When Matthew's Gospel tells of the arrival of Judas and the mob in the garden, Jesus' words to Judas are 'Friend, do what you are here to do' (Matthew 26:50). Why did Jesus not protect himself against the danger he knew he was in? We may gain some insight from the work of the 20th-century Swiss psychiatrist Carl Gustav Jung, who taught of the need for the human personality to 'embrace the shadow' on its journey towards wholeness and maturity. In doing so, the negative effects of what was perceived as evil would be transformed. It was through Jesus' willing acceptance of the evil in his midst and his refusal to shield himself against it that the resurrection to new life he brought to us through the cross became possible.

Reflection

Can you think of a time in life when 'embracing the shadow' of a situation brought about a transformation you would not have thought possible?

BARBARA MOSSE

A lesson in hospitality

Turning towards the woman, [Jesus] said to Simon [the Pharisee], 'Do you see this woman? I entered your house; you gave me no water for my feet, but she has bathed my feet with her tears and dried them with her hair. You gave me no kiss, but from the time I came in she has not stopped kissing my feet. You did not anoint my head with oil, but she has anointed my feet with ointment. Therefore, I tell you, her sins, which were many, have been forgiven; hence she has shown great love. But the one to whom little is forgiven, loves little.'

Even in the Middle East, it seems, where the hospitality code of honour was held in such high esteem, it was possible to do the job badly. If we read the entire passage (vv. 36–49), we will know that, prior to this startling incident, we are given no information about the hospitality Jesus had been offered by his host.

The woman who ministers to Jesus is classified as a sinner (often shorthand for a prostitute) by both the Gospel's writer (v. 37) and Jesus' host (v. 39). Simon the Pharisee's scorn for the woman prompts Jesus to catalogue his host's failures in hospitality: no water for washing his feet, no kiss and no oil for anointing. The woman, however, motivated by an instinctive love, spontaneously provided Jesus with all these things, whatever her past sins.

Simon the Pharisee gives us an object lesson in how not to offer hospitality and his shame is compounded by Jesus' publicly using the woman as a shining example of how to do it well. We like to think that we would never be guilty of Simon's lack of care, but can we honestly say that we have never encountered somebody whom we thought was not quite as 'good' as ourselves or a time when such a person—to our shame—has been held up to us as a model of a more Christlike way of being than we have shown?

Reflection

How open-hearted—or not—are our own experiences of offering hospitality? Can we identify our motives for offering hospitality to some and not to others?

BARBARA MOSSE

Look for no repayment

On one occasion when Jesus was going to the house of a leader of the Pharisees to eat a meal on the sabbath, they were watching him closely... He said also to the one who had invited him, 'When you give a luncheon or a dinner, do not invite your friends or your brothers or your relatives or rich neighbours, in case they may invite you in return, and you would be repaid. But when you give a banquet, invite the poor, the crippled, the lame and the blind. And you will be blessed, because they cannot repay you, for you will be repaid at the resurrection of the righteous.'

As we have seen, inviting Jesus for a meal often proved to be an uncomfortable experience for the host. This particular occasion began with Jesus controversially healing a man on the sabbath (vv. 1–6) and challenging his fellow guests over their desire for social precedence at the table (vv. 7–11). In our passage today, he turns his attention to his host, questioning the host's motives for inviting the people there.

Meals were important social ceremonies in that society, and the positions at table and the food served to different guests gave clear indications of each person's place in the pecking order. As so often happens, however, Jesus turns society's normal way of thinking and behaving on its head. Have nothing to do with this social discrimination and blatant self-interest, he says to his host. Instead, choose to invite those who have no way of inviting you back or repaying you in any way: 'invite the poor, the crippled, the lame, the blind'. Expect a heavenly, not earthly, reward.

To what degree can we allow Jesus' words to challenge our own attitudes to hospitality? How often can our dealings with others be truly said to be disinterested? All this may be easier said than done, perhaps, but Jesus' words offer a real possibility of liberation from our society's vicious and damaging circle of competition for power and esteem.

Reflection

'So whenever you give alms... do not let your left hand know what your right hand is doing, so that your alms may be done in secret; and your Father who sees in secret will reward you' (Matthew 6:2–4).

BARBARA MOSSE

They will hunger no more

Then one of the elders [said], 'Who are these, robed in white, and where have they come from?... These are they who have come out of the great ordeal; they have washed their robes and made them white in the blood of the Lamb. For this reason they are before the throne of God, and worship him day and night within his temple, and the one who is seated on the throne will shelter them. They will hunger no more, and thirst no more; the sun will not strike them, nor any scorching heat; for the Lamb at the centre of the throne will be their shepherd, and he will guide them to springs of the water of life.'

This passage appears to have been written against a background of the persecution of the fledgling Christian church. Under these concentrated and vindictive attacks, the writer makes clear that neither the physical nor the spiritual well-being of God's people can be guaranteed. What is promised, however, is that the sustaining, nurturing support of the Lamb of God will be with them, whatever ordeals each believer may be called on to withstand. The terms used here suggest hospitality at its best: food and drink, enough (but not too much) warmth, and protection, 'for the Lamb at the centre of the throne will be their shepherd' (v. 17).

There are echoes here of scriptures that would have been familiar to people at the time and continue to offer encouragement to us today. The Shepherd-Lamb who guides believers to the water of life had a clear influence on Jesus' own teaching (John 4:14; 10:11) and links strongly with Psalm 23 (which also reassures the believer of God's presence in the shadow of death) and Ezekiel 34:15 (God promises that he himself will be the shepherd of his sheep). The vision of hunger and thirst satisfied resonates with Old Testament prophecies of a future time when God will provide a feast for his people and suffering will be no more (Isaiah 25:6–10).

Reflection

'What no eye has seen, nor ear heard, nor the human heart conceived, what God has prepared for those who love him'—these things God has revealed to us through the Spirit' (1 Corinthians 2:9–10).

BARBARA MOSSE

Some minor prophets

We are about to reach parts of the Bible that even *New Daylight* has not reached before, in a taster of Obadiah and Nahum, alongside the more familiar territory of Micah and Habakkuk—all classified among the twelve 'minor prophets' of the Old Testament. All the writers are impatient in a godly way with either Israel or its neighbours and this impatience reflects God's holiness 'too pure to behold evil' (Habakkuk 1:13) and its demands on both the nations and Israel at a time of tumult in the Middle East.

Obadiah, with just 21 verses, is the shortest book in the Old Testament and is well summarised by Psalm 137:7: 'Remember, O Lord, against the Edomites, the day of Jerusalem's fall.' This fall, in 587BC, and the gloating over it by Israel's southern neighbour, provide the context, though the last part of the prophecy speaks of universal judgement.

Micah is no less forceful a prophet but has the advantage of seven chapters, through which his character emerges more fully than Obadiah's can in his few verses. Like Amos, Micah is a country man, suspicious of town life and a civilisation that oppresses the weak. His call in 6:8 'to do justice, and to love kindness, and to walk humbly with your God' summarises the moral teaching of the Old Testament prophets. He is also famous for looking to a golden age with universal peace.

Nahum's book, like Obadiah's, is short and includes little personal history, although the poetry contained within it is magnificent. Nahum breathes God's passionate resentment of the godless imperial power of Assyria, expressed in the sacking of its capital Nineveh in 612BC, an event that brought widespread rejoicing among its vassals. This is very different from an earlier theology that saw Assyria as 'the rod of [God's] anger' (Isaiah 10:5).

In Habakkuk's three chapters, we can sense his character (as we could Micah's) as a 'wrestler with God' (Jerome). Like Job, he dares to question the way God runs the world and also gives an answer in 2:4 that is much taken up in the New Testament: 'the righteous live by their faith'. His late seventh-century BC prophecy refers to an oppressor, which could be either the Assyrians or Babylonians, and it ends with a canticle (3:1–19) used in our liturgy to this day.

John Twisleton

Deceptive security

Your proud heart has deceived you, you that live in the clefts of the rock, whose dwelling is in the heights. You say in your heart, 'Who will bring me down to the ground?' Though you soar aloft like the eagle, though your nest is set among the stars, from there I will bring you down, says the Lord.

Have you ever visited the Middle East? You may have had some worries about the current security situation, depending on the stories in the media coverage at the time. I am privileged to have visited both Israel and Jordan, so am aware of the close proximity of the ancient rock ravines of Petra in Jordan to southern Israel. To reach Jerusalem from there is not straightforward, though, as you have to cross from one nation to another.

The Edomites, based in those impressive ravines, were always at loggerheads with the Israelites—an enmity said to go back to the falling out of Esau and Jacob. When the Assyrians conquered Jerusalem in 587BC, the Edomites swept north to occupy some of Israel's former territory, which gives the context for this first section of Obadiah's prophecy.

God's words against the Edomites pick up on the geography of what is now Petra: 'Your proud heart has deceived you, you that live in the clefts of the rock, whose dwelling is in the heights' (v. 3). This highly secure base, approached by a mile-long gorge with cliffs over 90 metres (300 feet) high, was eventually overrun by Nabatean Arabs in 312BC.

Obadiah traces Edom's downfall to a 'proud heart' that thought itself invulnerable. The Edomites are not heard of today, even though many other biblical groups live on. Pride is the deadliest of all sins since it hardens the heart so that we are cut off from God and people. The images of rock in this passage speak of the deceptive security of pride, be it national or individual.

Prayer

Lord, you said everyone who hears your words and acts on them will be like a wise man who built his house on rock. As we ponder your words through Obadiah, we see that our ultimate security is built on something better than rock. Heaven and earth will pass away, but your words will endure for ever. Amen

JOHN TWISLETON

Truth striking home

For the day of the Lord is near against all the nations. As you have done, it shall be done to you; your deeds shall return on your own head. For as you have drunk on my holy mountain, all the nations around you shall drink; they shall drink and gulp down... But on Mount Zion there shall be those that escape, and it shall be holy; and the house of Jacob shall take possession of those who dispossessed them.

The choice of a particular people and nation as being key to God's purpose is part of the mysterious outworking of his providence. To this day, many would continue to view events in the Middle East as showing forth that mystery, in a place so linked to God's redeeming love. Such events can help to make us feel at home with Obadiah, who plays his part in communicating God's vindication of those who keep faith in him.

The second part of Obadiah mentions the coming 'day of the Lord', which is a phenomenon used in all the prophets' writings in two ways. One, very evident here, is as God's triumphant vindication of Israel against enemies such as the people of Edom. Another, as in Amos, is God's judgement against Israel herself, on account of her unfaithfulness. Verse 15 speaks in the first sense of a day 'against all the nations', widening its horizon beyond the Edom-focused first part of the prophecy.

The day of the Lord spells doom for Israel's oppressors, but, reading scripture as a whole, we notice that it spells a day of doom for unfaithful Israelites. When Obadiah 17 speaks of 'those that escape', it touches on the self-understanding that grew in Israel after the exile, of being a faithful remnant, the seed of a new Israel.

God is Lord of history, the prophets remind us, and he can write straight through crooked lines. He is also Lord of our lives, so he both overcomes our enemies and uses them to deepen our humility.

Reflection

God's choice of me is no less wonderful than that of the Jewish nation. How much does my acceptance of that choice guide the way I live my life?

JOHN TWISLETON

Melting mountains

For lo, the Lord is coming out of his place, and will come down and tread upon the high places of the earth. Then the mountains will melt under him and the valleys will burst open, like wax near the fire, like waters poured down a steep place. All this is for the transgression of Jacob and for the sins of the house of Israel. What is the transgression of Jacob? Is it not Samaria? And what is the high place of Judah? Is it not Jerusalem?

The prophet Micah sees God shaking the land and releasing molten mountains in judgement against both the kingdoms of Israel and Judah and their capital towns of Samaria and Jerusalem because of their idolatry and exploitation of the poor.

We know more about the origins of earthquakes and volcanoes than they did in the seventh century BC but it doesn't stop our being in awe of or terrified by them. That knowledge shows us how the development of life on earth was served by the minerals released from the planet's interior by the motion of the tectonic plates. Earthquakes and lava can bring blessings; Micah saw them as God's wake-up call to his faithless people.

We are but a small part of the natural world God made, although his purpose for us is to lift us to just 'lower than God' (Psalm 8:5) by placing his Spirit in us so that we share his very own life. Micah demonstrates both God's frustration with the shortfall of humankind and his intention to deal with it by sending a Saviour to bring that life of God right into the human heart.

The palaeontologist, geologist and priest Teilhard de Chardin (1881–1955) saw in the coming of the Holy Spirit at the Eucharist an echo of both God's desire to 'bring fire to the earth' (Luke 12:49) and of molten lava that energises the earth's development.

Reflection

In the lifting up of the consecrated bread and wine in the Eucharist, Teilhard saw an anticipation of the raising up of Jesus as the 'Omega Point', when he returns to gather all things to himself. That golden future is first spoken of by Micah and his fellow prophets.

John Twisleton

Divine empowerment

Therefore it shall be night to you, without vision, and darkness to you, without revelation... the seers shall be disgraced, and the diviners put to shame; they shall all cover their lips, for there is no answer from God. But as for me, I am filled with power, with the spirit of the Lord, and with justice and might, to declare to Jacob his transgression and to Israel his sin.

While you are reading *New Daylight* for daily inspiration, millions will follow the more questionable practice of reading their daily horoscope. Divining the future is condemned again and again in the Bible and, in these verses, the prophet Micah draws a contrast between himself, inspired by the Spirit of the Lord, and the ungodly seers of his day.

How do you distinguish a true prophet from a false one? 'Events, dear boy', to somewhat misuse Harold Macmillan's reputed answer to the question of what he most feared as a politician. We see Micah's prophecy as part of the canon of scripture that is, overall, a witness to the events of the coming, death, resurrection and promised return of Jesus Christ who fulfils the prophetic writings. Even before the coming of Jesus, the Jewish people treasured Micah's writings as being from God, reading them as a continuous challenge to address injustice among themselves.

The Israelites recognised breath and wind as signs of the power of God, the life-giver. They also held that God's Spirit came on certain individuals so they could speak God's words of encouragement and challenge to the whole community. The contrast in these verses is between the seers and diviners covering their lips in shame and Micah's plain and open speaking for God. The community of faith came to agree that he was a true prophet for what he said had a force behind it that the seers lacked—and he pointed correctly to God's future.

Reflection

Through repentance, faith and baptism, we are 'filled with power, with the spirit of the Lord, and with justice and might'. How is the Holy Spirit working in my life and leading me to address injustice around me with his empowerment?

John Twisleton

Directing strength

He shall judge between many peoples, and shall arbitrate between strong nations far away; they shall beat their swords into plough-shares, and their spears into pruning-hooks; nation shall not lift up sword against nation, neither shall they learn war any more; but they shall all sit under their own vines and under their own fig trees, and no one shall make them afraid; for the mouth of the Lord of hosts has spoken.

This passage, which has parallels in Isaiah 2:4 and Joel 3:10, is a prophecy that has sounded down the ages and must be one of the most familiar texts of the Old Testament. The beating of swords into plough-shares is a creative image depicted, for example, in a statue at the United Nations headquarters in New York. It also appears in the final chorus of the musical *Les Miserables*, which sings of an ultimate freedom in which people will follow the plough and put away the sword.

Metals have been known about for around 9000 years, and iron for approximately 3000 years. A few hundred years before Micah's day, people discovered that, by adding a little charcoal to iron, they could produce a strong, hard alloy—steel. The prophets who spoke into the moral life of the community contrasted the right and wrong use of power, which is symbolised here in the creation of swords and ploughs. Both devices exploited a powerful resource, one directed to bloodshed and the other to agriculture and the sustaining of life.

We see the prophets speaking truth to power and, in so doing, they affirm God's purpose for human strength as being one that is directed to the common good rather than destruction. The contrasting of swords and ploughs, both made of metal, is updated in the current debate about bombs and power stations, both of which employ nuclear fuel. In both cases, the employment of something neutral in itself is made a good or bad instrument by mortal users.

Reflection

Think of the strengths you have—humour, intellect, sympathy and so on—and how they are employed. How might they be better directed to the service of God and the benefit of those around you?

JOHN TWISLETON

Bethlehem of noblest cities

You, O Bethlehem of Ephrathah, who are one of the little clans of Judah, from you shall come forth for me one who is to rule in Israel, whose origin is from of old, from ancient days. Therefore he shall give them up until the time when she who is in labour has brought forth; then the rest of his kindred shall return to the people of Israel. And he shall stand and feed his flock in the strength of the Lord, in the majesty of the name of the Lord his God. And they shall live secure, for now he shall be great to the ends of the earth.

The familiarity of this passage is due to its widespread use in carol services, since it predicts the coming of a Saviour from Bethlehem. These verses were 800 years old when Jesus would have heard them in the synagogue at Nazareth. We read in the Gospels how the parents of Jesus were taken away from Nazareth, where his birth was first announced to his mother, so she could give birth to him in the place five miles south of Jerusalem that Micah had indicated: Bethlehem of Ephrathah.

The Messiah is to be shepherd of Israel, for he shall stand and feed his flock in the strength of the Lord—and not only of Israel, for he shall be great to the ends of the earth. That care, provided from God, is to be a source of security so that all the changes and chances of history will not shake his people from him.

In three verses we find key pointers to the character of Jesus Christ—his birth in obscurity as one who bears humility, his coming in fulfilment of God's plan, his commitment to the care of individuals, his gift of eternal security and his universal appeal. His coming to Bethlehem, foretold by Micah, shows the consistency there is in the working of God, whose plan for his Son's coming was formed above and beyond history.

Reflection

Bethlehem, of noblest cities, none can once with thee compare; thou alone the Lord from heaven didst for us incarnate bear.

Aurelius Clemens Prudentius (348–410, trans. Edward Caswall, c.1849)

John Twisleton

Sacrifice and love

'With what shall I come before the Lord, and bow myself before God on high? Shall I come before him with burnt-offerings, with calves a year old? Will the Lord be pleased with thousands of rams, with tens of thousands of rivers of oil? Shall I give my firstborn for my transgression, the fruit of my body for the sin of my soul?' He has told you, O mortal, what is good; and what does the Lord require of you but to do justice, and to love kindness, and to walk humbly with your God?

All through the Bible and church history, there is creative tension between the institutional and the charismatic. In the Old Testament, it is represented in the contrasting writings associated with priests and prophets. In the New Testament it finds expression in Paul's affirmation that the church should be 'built upon the foundation of the apostles and prophets' (Ephesians 2:20). Whereas priests and apostles are institutional leaders within God's people, prophets always have a less comfortable standing, with their repeated and necessary wake-up calls.

The Old Testament sacrificial system expressed the duty of creatures towards their Creator that was fulfilled in the death of Christ and the living memorial of the Eucharist. Micah lists the different types of sacrifices—burnt offerings, cereal offerings with oil and the barbarous child sacrifices, condemned in the Law of Moses but not unknown in Israel. The prophet is one with his eighth-century contemporaries Amos, Hosea and Isaiah in affirming godliness as a response to God's love, which is lacking whenever sacrifices are made merely as a duty, let alone as a bribe!

'Do justice… love kindness… walk humbly with your God' (v. 8). Without these qualities, especially in leaders, any institution is set to founder, from family up to nation. Through the Christian centuries, this sentence from Micah has demonstrated the power of God's word to shake the foundations of society, as in Martin Luther King's use of them to challenge the racism of his day and renew American society.

Reflection

It is not the magnitude of our actions but the amount of love that is put into them that matters.

Teresa of Calcutta (1910–1997)

John Twisleton

Nahum 1:1–3 (NRSV)

God confounds our enemies

An oracle concerning Nineveh. The book of the vision of Nahum of Elkosh. A jealous and avenging God is the Lord, the Lord is avenging and wrathful; the Lord takes vengeance on his adversaries and rages against his enemies. The Lord is slow to anger but great in power, and the Lord will by no means clear the guilty.

The authority of scripture is balanced by that of the church as interpreter. Within scripture, we also need to avoid reading just what we like and setting some texts above others. Today we are looking at the neglected book of Nahum to see how it serves as part of God's word for us today.

Though Nahum's name (v. 1) means 'God consoles', the consolation he offers in his magnificent poetry is rather one-sided. It is consolation for Israel at the expense of her Assyrian oppressor, through the well-chronicled sack of Nineveh by the Babylonians in 612BC, detailed as part of this prophecy. Other prophets, such as Isaiah and Micah, see the Babylonians as God's instrument for correcting Israel as well as Assyria, so we need to recognise Nahum as one voice among many.

It is consoling, though, to see one's enemies confounded! The biblical history we are part of is, in a deep sense, 'his story', in which God discomfits Israel's enemies, from the Egyptian Pharaoh to the military steamroller of Assyria. With Christ's coming, the universal enemy of humanity is defeated, so Paul can say, 'Where, O death, is your victory?' (1 Corinthians 15:55), mirroring Nahum's celebration of Assyria's downfall.

'The Lord takes vengeance on his adversaries and rages against his enemies. The Lord is slow to anger but great in power' (Nahum 1:2–3). As we face things or people we know to be wrong, we need to stand firm with godly patience, strengthened by God's word, given to us by Nahum, that points to the ultimate triumph of goodness.

Prayer

O Lord, raise up, we pray, your power and come among us, and with great might succour us; that whereas, through our sins and wickedness we are grievously hindered… your bountiful grace and mercy may speedily help and deliver us; through Jesus Christ your Son our Lord.

Collect for the Second Sunday of Advent, *Common Worship*
John Twisleton

Overpowering lions

Devastation, desolation, and destruction! Hearts faint and knees tremble, all loins quake, all faces grow pale! What became of the lions' den, the cave of the young lions, where the lion goes, and the lion's cubs, with no one to disturb them? The lion has torn enough for his whelps and strangled prey for his lionesses; he has filled his caves with prey and his dens with torn flesh. See, I am against you, says the Lord of hosts, and I will burn your chariots in smoke, and the sword shall devour your young lions.

This mocking passage picks up on the lion image that was so commonly used in Assyrian civilisation, associated with sculpture and inscriptions from the period 700 years before Christ that still abound in museums. The lions' den was Nineveh and the prophecy that 'the sword shall devour your young lions' refers to the way the returning Assyrian armies would find the nation's capital, Nineveh, despoiled. This conquest by the Babylonians can be accurately dated to 612BC.

Nahum's near contemporary Hosea writes how 'the Lord... roars like a lion; when he roars, his children shall come trembling' (11:10). The lion image is also attributed to the Son of God, Jesus Christ, of whom John wrote, 'the Lion of the tribe of Judah, the Root of David, has conquered' (Revelation 5:5). These passages centre on physical power, of which the lion is the most potent natural symbol, and make an analogy with divine power and authority over both individuals and nations.

In his prophecy, Nahum points to the spectacular fall of Assyria as the work of a higher power intent on establishing his rule on earth by choosing a particular nation that is to be vindicated in world history. This vindication was to come especially through the advent of the Lion of Judah, who is also 'the Lamb of God who takes away the sin of the world' (John 1:29).

Reflection

As you follow today's round of news, in whatever media, pray that, through the unfolding of powerful world events, God will work in your prayer, so that 'The kingdom of the world has become the kingdom of our Lord and of his Messiah' (Revelation 11:15).

JOHN TWISLETON

Looking God in the eyes

Are you not from of old, O Lord my God, my Holy One? You shall not die. O Lord, you have marked them for judgement; and you, O Rock, have established them for punishment. Your eyes are too pure to behold evil, and you cannot look on wrongdoing; why do you look on the treacherous, and are silent when the wicked swallow those more righteous than they?

How can God, with 'eyes too pure to behold evil... look on wrongdoing... when the wicked swallow those more righteous than they?' (v. 13). The prophet Habakkuk may be a prophet, but he is also a sceptic. He speaks God's word, but also questions it. He has a particular resonance with our own sceptical culture, which, used to getting an answer for everything, baulks at unanswerable questions, using them to fuel disbelief in God.

How can an all-seeing holy God but be affronted by unrighteousness, the prophet muses. We could pause with Habakkuk to reflect on God's 'eyes too pure to behold evil' (v. 13) and the affront to them of the evil in us. As Christians, we are aware of God's love for us as his beloved children, but we are also aware of the sin that is in us. Although Christ is in us, delightful to his Father, there is also the sin that affronts his holiness. Like truant children having to look a good parent in the eye, we sense the pain our selfishness gives our heavenly Father.

In the Christian interpretation, all scripture is to be read in the light of Jesus Christ, so that the pain of a holy God at the sight of sin, prophesied by Habakkuk, is expressed and absorbed in Christ's passion and crucifixion. God's righteous judgement on sin is pronounced over Jesus, our beloved substitute, who dies in our place to live in our place by the Spirit. His death is a mysterious act of substitution—of the innocent for the guilty—and also expresses what sin is and what it does to God, as noted by Habakkuk.

Reflection

'For our sake he made him to be sin who knew no sin, so that in him we might become the righteousness of God' (2 Corinthians 5:21).

JOHN TWISLETON

Pride: source of malfunction

Look at the proud! Their spirit is not right in them, but the right-eous live by their faith. Moreover, wealth is treacherous; the arro-gant do not endure. They open their throats wide as Sheol; like Death they never have enough.

The opening dialogue of Habakkuk, between the prophet and God in chapter 1, questions respectfully how God rules the world and points to the vexed issue of evil. It seems to him that God is punishing evildo-ers among his people by letting loose even greater evildoers, despite having 'eyes too pure to behold evil' (see yesterday's notes).

God's answer comes loud and clear in chapter 2 and it points to human pride as the main obstacle to human understanding: 'Look at the proud! Their spirit is not right in them, but the righteous live by their faith' (v. 4). It requires a right spirit to discern the hand of God as it works for good through both good and bad circumstances.

This verse is picked up in the New Testament writings of Paul and the letter to the Hebrews, with reference to faith as trust in God, which justifies us in his sight, rather than slavish obedience to precepts. Habakkuk's understanding of faith is, in fact, more like faithfulness to God and the law and also a spiritual steadfastness concerning them, in the face of things that might provoke disloyalty. It is faith shown in perseverance through suffering that is detailed in Hebrews 11—in other words, nothing notional or sentimental but an ongoing decision to walk with God in all circumstances.

The way we look at life is affected by body, mind and spirit, espe-cially the collaboration of the last two. A brilliant mind, however search-ing, will be distracted from seeing how things really are unless there is also humility of spirit. Such humility flows from Habakkuk, even as he puts his arguments, and Bible scholar Jerome therefore honoured him with the title 'wrestler with God'.

Reflection

There are things in my life that I struggle with. Some will be wrong, which I will need help in overcoming. Others will require steadfastness, so that I live cheerfully with unresolved matters to the best of my ability.

JOHN TWISLETON

The power of praise

Though the fig tree does not blossom, and no fruit is on the vines; though the produce of the olive fails and the fields yield no food; though the flock is cut off from the fold and there is no herd in the stalls, yet I will rejoice in the Lord; I will exult in the God of my salvation.

If Habakkuk's theology links to Job (see the introduction to this set of readings), his poetry links to the Psalms, and so his little book ends with a canticle used in worship to this very day. The so-called 'Prayer of Habakkuk' moves from exalting God in creation, especially in times of trouble, to describing how, through the gift of faith, even hunger and misery can be overcome as we put our trust in the Lord. The biblical writers speak out of age-old human contexts, and this passage has retained its power through generations afflicted by famine and loss of livelihood. It is a passage that recounts hardship, but immediately calls for a change of focus, a lifting of the heart and mind to God in praise.

The Old Testament prophets are essential companions to the priestly writers and psalmists in waking people up to essentials—in worship, for example. To give God praise conditional on his provision of material things is, as Habakkuk vividly reminds us, failing to praise God for who he is in himself, because this is the very heart of praise. God is worthy of praise in himself, although it is good to thank him for all he provides us with.

'I will exult in the God of my salvation': this salvation is not a relationship of equals. God's extraordinary choice of mortals is balanced by our recognition of God as a God whose workings no mortal mind can encompass. Through the coming of Jesus and his suffering for us, Habakkuk's proclamation of God's worthiness of praise in the sight of evil gains even deeper force and depth.

Reflection

Whereas petitionary prayer and thanksgiving usually relate to gifts from God, praise is arguably a higher form of prayer, since its focus is on God for who he is in himself rather than for what he gives us.

JOHN TWISLETON

The Gift of Years

Supporting
The Gift of Years
with a gift in your will

For many charities, income from legacies is crucial in enabling them to plan ahead, and often provides the funding to develop new projects. A legacy to support BRF's ministry would make a huge difference.

As we're living longer, BRF's The Gift of Years (www.thegiftofyears.org.uk) celebrates the blessings of long life—but it doesn't underestimate the difficulties. As more and more churches seek to respond to the challenges of an ageing population, The Gift of Years signposts practical ways in which our later years can be infinitely more fulfilling, intense and rewarding.

The vision and purpose of The Gift of Years is:

- to resource the spiritual journey of older people.
- to resource ministry among older people, wherever they may be—in congregations, in care homes or in their own homes.
- to emphasise the opportunities that greater longevity brings, so that our later years might be some of the most spiritually fertile years of our earthly life.
- to encourage and enable younger generations to consider what constitutes 'successful ageing' and so prepare for more positive experiences in older age.
- to 'join up the dots' to make more widely known the wealth of resources and courses already available and the organisations and individuals working in this field.

Throughout its history, BRF's ministry has been enabled thanks to the generosity of those who have shared its vision and supported its work, both by giving during their lifetime and also through legacy gifts.

A legacy gift would help fund the development and sustainability of BRF's The Gift of Years into the future. We hope you may consider a legacy gift to help us continue to take this work forward.

For further information about making a gift to BRF in your will or to discuss how a specific bequest could be used to develop our ministry, please contact Sophie Aldred (Head of Fundraising) or Richard Fisher (Chief Executive) by email at fundraising@brf.org.uk or by phone on 01865 319700.

The BRF

Magazine

Celebrating 20 years of Barnabas for Children

Olivia Warburton

When BRF's Barnabas Children's Ministry is mentioned, what comes to mind for you? Is it our successful schools programme of Barnabas RE Days and INSET, our Barnabas in Churches website teeming with creative ideas, or our range of published resources, developed over the past 20 years?

In 1995, four years after BRF made the decision to start producing books as well as Bible reading notes, the Barnabas imprint was launched. Over the years, highlights have included titles as varied as Jenny Hyson's *The Easter Garden: Following in the Footsteps of Jesus*, Margaret Withers' *Welcome to the Lord's Table* course book for Communion preparation, the primary school resources *Stories for Interactive Assemblies* and *Stories of Everyday Saints*, and our edition of Anno Domini's *My First Bible*.

Barnabas began with a focus on publishing books for children under eleven, and our range of colour gift books continues to grow, with picture story books, sticker books and children's Bibles. Look out for the lavishly illustrated *Barnabas 365 Story Bible*, available from this February.

It then became apparent that there was a need to equip those working with children, both in churches and schools. On the schools side,

we now produce classroom material for RE teachers and Collective Worship resources that also have strong take-up by church visitors leading assemblies in schools. Our new publication *RE in the Classroom with 4–5s*, by Helen Jaeger, offers biblically based lesson plans for use with an age group for whom there is currently a shortage of appropriate RE teaching material.

We also produce a wide range of material for churches, increasingly with an eye to an all-age context alongside more traditional children's groups. *Creative Ideas for Lent and Easter* by Jane

Tibbs provides a wealth of seasonal activities for different ages and interests, and coming soon is *50 Praise, Pray and Play Sessions* by Rona Orme, providing easy-to-run all-age outlines for use throughout the week with families in the community. We are also respected providers of training resources for children's workers, as well as curriculum material for key moments in the spiritual journey such as baptism and confirmation.

Another key area of activity within Barnabas for Children is in encouraging and supporting faith in the home. Our new title *Exploring God's Love in Everyday Life* by Yvonne Morris, a follow-up to *Side by Side with God in Everyday Life*, offers 20 readings, reflections and prayers based on 1 Corinthians 13 for parents and children to share together.

On a larger scale, our new *Barnabas Family Bible*, developed in partnership with Bible Society, takes families right the way through the Bible story, helping them to share a reflective and interactive time together through Bible story extracts, comments, questions, prayer and activity ideas, visual aids, key verses and Old and New Testament story links. James Catford, Group Chief Executive of Bible Society, writes:

Bible Society believes that every child has the right to experience the Bible for themselves and that's why we're excited to be partnering with BRF in the publication of The Barnabas Family Bible. *This book encourages families to sit and explore the riches of the Bible together, reading the Bible text of 110 popular stories while delving deeper through activities, questions and prayers. Millions of people around the world have grown up with the Bible stories. It is our hope that* The Barnabas Family Bible *will enable families to keep the Bible alive for another generation.*

Children's and family ministry is changing fast, and, as we continue to respond to the needs across our churches and in our homes, there is much that is both exciting and challenging as we look ahead. Our hope is that we can indeed help children and adults alike to keep the Bible alive for another generation… and beyond!

Olivia Warburton is Commissioning Editor for Barnabas books for Children and Families, and author of Teaching Narnia: A cross-curricular classroom and assembly resource for RE teachers *(Barnabas in Schools, 2013).*

Guidelines 30th anniversary

David Spriggs

'Where's the birthday cake?' Yesterday I was at my grandson's party! Yes, excitement, presents and people young and old may be important to commemorate a birthday when you are seven instead of six, but the cake is essential. Of course, parents and grandparents are not only sharing the excitement but are also grateful for the privilege of seeing a young life unfold.

Unfortunately I can't offer you any birthday cake but I am pleased that I can invite you to our celebration. In this issue we are celebrating not seven but 30 years of *Guidelines*, and we can all be both excited and grateful. We're excited that, in spite of all the pressures on publishing, reading and especially Bible reading, BRF had the foresight and courage to start this new venture in 1985 and it is still going strong. We know from emails and letters, as well as the number of copies published, that *Guidelines* meets a real need and benefits people in many areas of Christian life today. We are therefore grateful to God for calling BRF into this venture and for linking people with this resource. We invite you to share this sense of gratitude with us.

To help us all, let's consider more precisely what we are celebrating. After all, there are many notes available from BRF and other providers—but *Guidelines* offers something unique in the regular Bible reading notes marketplace. Its primary intention is to 'enable all its readers to interpret and apply the biblical text with confidence in today's world, while helping to equip church leaders as they meet the challenge of mission and disciple-building'.

At the heart of *Guidelines* is not the notes but the Bible. Over a four- to five-year period we aim to cover most of the New Testament, and the Old Testament in seven to eight years. Stimulating people to engage with the scriptures is our vital task, but it is not *our* selection, and not the 'comfortable' words alone. We recognise that all of scripture is God's gift to his people, not just the easier sections.

Before we can 'interpret and apply' the Bible, we need to engage with it appropriately. This appropriate 'deeper' engagement is what *Guidelines* exists for, and, to facilitate it, we seek out the best biblical scholars to illuminate the text with both their knowledge and their profound faith. Many of the contributions come from people who are working on major new commentaries. I am constantly surprised that these very busy scholars are prepared to accept the challenge of condensing their own work into manageable 'chunks' for us. There are very few who refuse an invitation to write for us, and that is because of the excellent reputation that Guidelines has earned during 30 thirty years. In no small measure, this is due to the hard work and inspiration of its different editors and contributors over that time.

We recognise, too, that scripture is the core text of all the churches. We seek to reflect this by including writers whose spiritual homes are in all the main traditions, especially the Anglican one but also the Roman Catholic, the Free Churches and the newer emerging streams. Most of our writers are thoroughly immersed in the challenges of living out our faith today and the worship and mission of these churches. Many of them work in higher level theological education, but we also include people whose main focus is their local church or diocesan work. Interpreting the Bible involves praxis as well as study, and such writers have a particularly valuable contribution to make by providing notes that focus on mission, leadership and discipleship.

Recently a large survey of 400,000 individuals and 1500 churches attempted to discern what drives spiritual growth ('growing in love of God and love of others'). The survey found that there were many factors at different levels of maturation. However, reflection on scripture was the only catalyst that appeared at every level. An article summarising the research for the Centenary of the Edinburgh Conference of 2010 ends with the following challenge:

Spiritually vibrant churches have spiritually vibrant leaders... Do you take time to reflect on Scripture for yourself, apart from preparing to teach, lead a group, or preach a sermon? Are you cultivating a passion for God's Word that is contagious?

N.S. LEWIS, 'LESSONS LEARNED FROM THE REVEAL SPIRITUAL LIFE SURVEY' IN *BIBLE IN MISSION* (REGNUM, 2013), P. 263

Incisive and illuminating insights into the biblical text are at the core of *Guidelines* but, in the end, if the Bible is not transforming us, then it is failing to perform its role. Eugene Peterson, the author of *THE MESSAGE*, has some deeply challenging things to say to us here: 'There is no word of God that God does not intend to be lived by us... every word of

God revealed and read in the Bible is there to be conceived and born in us' (*Eat This Book*, Hodder and Stoughton, 2006, p. 114). Here again, *Guidelines* seeks to keep the Bible, not the writers' notes or the reader's response, at the heart of this process. There is immense transformative power in the scriptures, properly understood. We hope that the notes, rather than rushing readers to personal introspection, will encourage them to stick to the scriptures, allowing God's word to work on their minds and imaginations, their wills and behaviour.

Of course, this is neither an automatic nor an enforced transformation; rather (again, in the words of Peterson), 'God doesn't make us do any of this: God's word is personal address, inviting, commanding, challenging, rebuking, judging, comforting, directing. But not forcing… We are given space and freedom to answer, to enter into the conversation' (*Eat This Book*, p. 109). So at the end of the week, the concluding 'Guidelines' section offers ways in which this process of transformation, through engagement with the text, can become more deeply rooted within us.

Guidelines, in other words, seeks to treat us as adults who can cope with the whole of scripture, who value the ongoing fruits of scholarship and are serious in working out our faith and life within both our culture and the churches of today. The notes both direct us to the Bible as central and seek to enable us to attend carefully and consistently to that centre. Equally, however, *Guidelines* acknowledges that we need the ongoing attention and renewal that comes to us from God through the Holy Spirit.

The transformative work of scripture is not limited to the individual or even Christian communities. Ultimately, scripture is (in Lesslie Newbigin's words) 'the story of the world', so *Guidelines* helps us to apply scripture to our world—or, perhaps better, helps us to 'see' the world through a transformed imagination and then join with God in his mission.

It is with deep appreciation of the contribution of *Guidelines* in 'unfolding' scripture that I invite you to celebrate its 30th birthday with me, to offer praise to God for all it has achieved and to pray for an increasing and effective role for *Guidelines* in the future.

Your decrees are wonderful… The unfolding of your word gives light. (Psalm 119:129–130, NRSV)

David Spriggs is a Baptist minister who has worked for the last 15 years with Bible Society, helping the churches and Higher Education to engage more fruitfully with the Bible.

Recommended reading

Kevin Ball

One of the biggest headaches for parents of teenagers is convincing them that parents do have a bit of wisdom to pass on that is valuable. But is it just teens who are so difficult to persuade? As human beings, we seem have a 'standard operating procedure' which dictates that we value knowledge only if we have discovered it for ourselves rather than by embracing the hard-won experience of others.

What about issues of faith? Personal discovery is vital for any true, deep relationship with God to grow, but there is also so much that can be learnt from past travellers if we care to look. Prayer is one of the areas in which many people struggle. John Twisleton offers help in his new book *Using the Jesus Prayer*, unwrapping from his personal experience the value of this very ancient prayer, a prayer well known by name but perhaps not so well known in practice as a key step to contemplation.

Fiona Stratta's first book for BRF, *Walking with Gospel Women* (2012), was a bestseller, helping individuals and groups to enter the world of New Testament women through carefully crafted personal monologues that told of each woman's encounter with Jesus. Through her stories, Fiona enabled readers to feel the emotions, concerns and passions of these long-gone individuals—to walk in their shoes and discover that, despite the passing of time, their emotions were very similar to ours today and can offer effective, relevant help for our Christian journey. In her new book, *Walking with Old Testament Women*, Fiona turns her attention to women even further away from us in time but still powerfully able to pass on wisdom in the life-issues that really matter.

Caroline George discovered the wisdom of age by leading a women's fellowship group. She found that, although advanced in years, the women had much to offer, and her times with the group became the catalyst for her new book, *Living Liturgies*, a resource for those leading and pastoring older generations.

Passing on our experience of faith is a key part of Christian witness.

We do that effectively at BRF through the ministry of Messy Church, which is reaching out around the world to unchurched families. Messy Churches need resourcing, and this month we publish two new books full of ideas: the *Messy Family Fun* holiday club programme and *Messy Easter*, which offers three complete Messy sessions for Lent, Holy Week and Easter.

You can keep up to date with all of our new titles and offers by signing up to the regular BRF email at www.brfonline.org.uk/enews-signup/

Using the Jesus Prayer
Steps to a simpler Christian life
John Twisleton

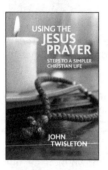

pb, 978 1 84101 778 5, 128 pages, £6.99

How can I live a simpler Christian life? Is there a summary of faith that's clear, memorable and portable? An effective, biblically based guide to praying at all times? An aid that can restore inner peace amid the busyness and the noise of daily life, to bring communion with God?

'Yes,' says parish priest John Twisleton. John has used the Jesus Prayer for many years and, in this new book, he shares his experience of its use, so that you may also enjoy its rich treasure.

John begins the book by reflecting on the good news intrinsic to the Jesus Prayer, and goes on to show how the spiritual discipline of repeating the prayer is built upon its base in scripture. He then changes gear to look at how the methods used to combat anxiety and mental distraction in popular Eastern 'mindfulness' exercises can be found in the Jesus Prayer as a 'God-given mantra'. The book concludes with practical advice about saying the Jesus Prayer, how it helps in relating worship to life, and its usefulness in building up the integrity of Christian believers.

Walking with Old Testament Women
More interactive Bible meditations
Fiona Stratta

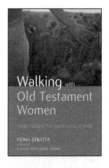

pb, 978 1 84101 718 1, 176 pages, £7.99

Superficially, women today may seem very different from the women of the Old Testament who lived so long ago, but, as we hear their stories, we discover that we have much in common: joy and heartache, love and jealousy, difficult choices and the need for patience, wisdom and courage. In our wider society, too, there are dysfunctional families beset by difficulties, and many women across the world have little personal choice or freedom.

Fiona Stratta, author of the BRF bestselling book *Walking with Gospel Women*, provides 21 imaginative, Ignatian-style monologues and studies based on the biblical accounts of Old Testament women including Sarah, Ruth, Bathsheba, Hannah and Tamar. Each character tells her own story. Fiona provides points for reflection and discussion after each monologue, enabling issues to be explored and links to New Testament teaching made. Of greatest importance, we see in these narratives God's wonderful grace, his undeserved favour and blessing, touching the lives of these women, and discover that the same grace is available to us. Suitable for both group and individual use.

Living Liturgies
Transition time resources for services, prayer and conversation with older people
Caroline George

pb, 978 0 85746 323 4, 128 pages, £7.99

This is a creative and original book of liturgies and reflections for use in worship and pastoral ministry with older people, who are moving from the 'third age' to the more dependent 'fourth age' of life. Developed by the author after many years of working in church and community settings with older people, the book provides an invaluable resource for those embarking on this ministry as well as those wanting inspiration for their ongoing work. The book also includes wider reflections on ageing and spirituality.

Messy Family Fun
A five-day holiday club and one-day fun day for all the family!
Lucy Moore

pb, 978 0 85746 305 0, 96 pages, £9.99

Messy Family Fun provides a holiday club programme for the whole family or for children coming with an adult. It offers five consecutive days of two-hour sessions followed by a meal, reflecting the values of Messy Church (Christ-centred, creativity, celebration, hospitality, all-age), and includes background and principles for this model, alongside session plans, downloadable templates and follow-up ideas. There is also a one-day Messy Church Fun Day outline, which can be used as a trial run for the full holiday club and/or as a community event to attract new families.

Messy Easter
3 complete sessions and a treasure trove of craft ideas for Lent, Easter and Pentecost
Jane Leadbetter

pb, 978 1 84101 717 4, 96 pages, £5.99

Three complete sessions for Lent, Holy Week and Easter, together with a wealth of activities to extend the range of excitingly messy activities for your Messy Church, including creative prayers, games, food crafts and ideas for organising an Easter trail. Craft templates and a session planning grid are provided.

To order copies of any of these books, please turn to the order form on page 155, or visit www.brfonline.org.uk.

An extract from
Reflecting the Glory

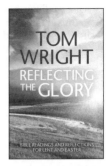

TOM
WRIGHT
REFLECTING
THE GLORY

BIBLE READINGS AND REFLECTIONS
FOR LENT AND EASTER

In BRF's Lent book for 2015 (first published in 1998), author Tom Wright draws on New Testament passages to show that through God's Holy Spirit, the suffering but also the glory of Christ can be incarnate in our lives, enabling us to be the people of God for the world. The following extract is a comment on John 13:1–20.

Jesus' 'hour' (v. 1) was the moment when he was going to accomplish the mission for which he had been sent into the world. John characterises this moment in terms of departing from the world and going to the Father, which is why the following chapters are known as the 'farewell discourses'… Still in the first verse of the passage, John says that Jesus had loved his followers 'to the end'. This phrase 'to the end' doesn't just mean that he went on loving them as long as there was breath in his body, although that was true as well. John clearly means that he loved them to the uttermost; there was nothing that love could do for them that he did not do for them. And this introduces us to the next scene, when Jesus enacts, symbolically, the love of God.

John notes that Judas, the son of Simon Iscariot, had already found it in his heart to betray Jesus. As betrayal involved an act of accusation, of accusing Jesus before the chief priests and the Jewish rulers, John attributes this betrayal to the devil, who in Hebrew has the name 'the Satan', which means 'the accuser'. Judas now personified the sense of accusation that had been hanging over Jesus for much of his ministry, and that was about to confront him openly. Verse 3, however, describes Jesus as knowing that the Father had given all things into his hands; he had come from God and was returning to God… He was committed to a course of action which was the very embodiment, or, to use the Latin-based word, the incarnation of the love of God.

After supper, to express that graphically, he got up from the table, took off his outer robe, tied a towel around himself, poured water into a basin and washed the disciples' feet. When John describes that sequence, he is describing not only the action of Jesus at the table but also the action of Jesus in coming down from God, laying aside the garments of glory, taking instead the form of a servant, girding himself with a towel and doing for his friends the work that a servant would normally do…

There follows a little scene of what might almost be called comedy. Peter misunderstands. He does not want Jesus washing his feet. But Jesus insists: 'You don't understand this at the moment,' he says to Peter, 'but you will later.' Peter goes on blustering: 'I'm not going to let you wash my feet.' And Jesus responds, rather sharply: 'If I don't wash you, you can have no part in me, no share in what I'm doing. You must let me wash you.' Peter's innate human pride means he doesn't want to be a humble leader. He might have to be humble in turn, and that would never do. But when he is faced with the threat that, unless he goes through with it, he won't have any part in Jesus' work, then, typically, he flips to the other extreme and says: 'You had better wash all of me—Lord, not my feet only but my hands and my head!' Jesus replies (v. 10), 'One who has bathed does not need to wash, except for the feet, but is entirely clean. And you are clean, though not all of you.' In other words, he has already accepted Peter; he has already cleaned him. But, as Peter walks through the world, his feet will get dirty again and once more need washing. In the same way, when we pray the Lord's Prayer we don't have to start every time as totally unforgiven sinners. We come as God's beloved children, saying 'Our Father in heaven', but halfway through the prayer we admit gladly and freely that we have some things that need sorting out, some problems that need addressing today. And it will be the same tomorrow.

So Jesus washes the disciples' feet, and explains to Peter what it means, how it connects with their sharing in his life, his glory, his work. When he has finished, put on his robe again and returned to the table, he explains further to them the significance of what he has done… Well, he says, you call me Teacher and Lord (v. 13), and you are right to do so, because that is what I am. You must learn, though, that if your Lord and Teacher has washed your feet, you also should wash one another's feet. Jesus is deliberately standing the normal social order on its head, turning the values of the world upside-down…

Throughout all this, Jesus is aware that one of those sitting at the table, one of those whose feet he has washed, is about to get up and leave the company, never to return. The only time they will see him again is when he appears in the garden to betray his master. Jesus is less concerned about that, however, than about conveying to his disciples the meaning of his actions. This is what it means to be equal with God, to reveal the glory of God. Loving his followers to the uttermost, he wants to bequeath them this new way of life which is no less than embodying the love of God—love that was expressed uniquely in Jesus, but then given by his Spirit to all his followers.

To order a copy of this book, please turn to the order form on page 155.

SUPPORTING BRF'S MINISTRY

As a Christian charity, BRF is involved in eight complementary areas.

- **BRF** (www.brf.org.uk) resources adults for their spiritual journey through Bible reading notes, books and Quiet Days. BRF also provides the infrastructure that supports our other specialist ministries.
- **Foundations21** (www.foundations21.net) provides flexible and innovative ways for individuals and groups to explore their Christian faith and discipleship through a multimedia internet-based resource.
- **Messy Church** (www.messychurch.org.uk), led by Lucy Moore, enables churches all over the UK (and increasingly abroad) to reach children and adults beyond the fringes of the church.
- **Barnabas in Churches** (www.barnabasinchurches.org.uk) helps churches to support, resource and develop their children's ministry with the under-11s more effectively .
- **Barnabas in Schools** (www.barnabasinschools.org.uk) enables primary school children and teachers to explore Christianity creatively and bring the Bible alive within RE and Collective Worship.
- **Faith in Homes** (www.faithinhomes.org.uk) supports families to explore and live out the Christian faith at home.
- **Who Let The Dads Out** (www.wholetthedadsout.org) inspires churches to engage with dads and their pre-school children.
- **The Gift of Years** (www.brf.org.uk/thegiftofyears) celebrates the blessings of long life and seeks to meet the spiritual needs of older people.

At the heart of BRF's ministry is a desire to equip adults and children for Christian living—helping them to read and understand the Bible, explore prayer and grow as disciples of Jesus. We need your help to make an impact on the local church, local schools and the wider community.

- You could support BRF's ministry with a one-off gift or regular donation (using the response form on page 153).
- You could consider making a bequest to BRF in your will.
- You could encourage your church to support BRF as part of your church's giving to home mission—perhaps focusing on a specific area of our ministry, or a particular member of our Barnabas team.
- Most important of all, you could support BRF with your prayers.

If you would like to discuss how a specific gift or bequest could be used in the development of our ministry, please phone 01865 319700 or email enquiries@brf.org.uk.

Whatever you can do or give, we thank you for your support.

NEW DAYLIGHT SUBSCRIPTIONS

Please note our subscription rates 2015–2016. From the May 2015 issue, the new subscription rates will be:

Individual subscriptions covering 3 issues for under 5 copies, payable in advance (including postage and packing):

	UK	Eur/Economy	Standard
NEW DAYLIGHT each set of 3 p.a.	£16.35	£24.00	£27.60
NEW DAYLIGHT 3-year sub (i.e. 9 issues) (Not available for Deluxe)	£42.75	N/A	N/A
NEW DAYLIGHT DELUXE each set of 3 p.a.	£20.70	£32.70	£37.95

Group subscriptions covering 3 issues for 5 copies or more, sent to ONE UK address (post free).

NEW DAYLIGHT	£12.90	each set of 3 p.a.
NEW DAYLIGHT DELUXE	£16.50	each set of 3 p.a.

Overseas group subscription rates available on request.
Contact enquiries@brf.org.uk.

Please note that the annual billing period for Group Subscriptions runs from 1 May to 30 April.

Copies of the notes may also be obtained from Christian bookshops:

NEW DAYLIGHT	£4.30 each copy
NEW DAYLIGHT DELUXE	£5.50 each copy

Visit www.biblereadingnotes.org.uk for information about our other Bible reading notes and Apple apps for iPhone and iPod touch.

BRF MINISTRY APPEAL RESPONSE FORM

I want to help BRF by funding some of its core ministries. Please use my gift for:
❏ Where most needed ❏ Barnabas Children's Ministry ❏ Foundations21
❏ Messy Church ❏ Who Let The Dads Out? ❏ The Gift of Years
Please complete all relevant sections of this form and print clearly.

Title ____ First name/initials _____ Surname _____

Address _____

_____ Postcode _____

Telephone _____ Email _____

Regular giving

If you would like to give by direct debit, please tick the box below and fill in details:

❏ I would like to make a regular gift of £ _____ per month / quarter / year
(delete as appropriate) by Direct Debit. (Please complete the form on page 159.)

If you would like to give by standing order, please contact Debra McKnight (tel: 01865 319700; email debra.mcknight@brf.org.uk; write to BRF address).

One-off donation

Please accept my special gift of
❏ £10 ❏ £50 ❏ £100 (other) £ _____ by

❏ Cheque / Charity Voucher payable to 'BRF'
❏ Visa / Mastercard / Charity Card
(delete as appropriate)

Name on card _____

Card no. ⟦ ⟧⟦ ⟧⟦ ⟧⟦ ⟧ ⟦ ⟧⟦ ⟧⟦ ⟧⟦ ⟧ ⟦ ⟧⟦ ⟧⟦ ⟧⟦ ⟧ ⟦ ⟧⟦ ⟧⟦ ⟧⟦ ⟧

Start date ⟦ ⟧⟦ ⟧ ⟦ ⟧⟦ ⟧   Expiry date ⟦ ⟧⟦ ⟧ ⟦ ⟧⟦ ⟧

Security code ⟦ ⟧⟦ ⟧⟦ ⟧

Signature _____ Date _____

❏ I would like to give a legacy to BRF. Please send me further information.

❏ I want BRF to claim back tax on this gift.
(If you tick this box, please fill in gift aid declaration overleaf.)

Please detach and send this completed form to: BRF, 15 The Chambers, Vineyard, Abingdon OX14 3FE. BRF is a Registered Charity (No.233280)

GIFT AID DECLARATION

Bible Reading Fellowship

Please treat as Gift Aid donations all qualifying gifts of money made
today ☐   in the past 4 years ☐   in the future ☐ (tick all that apply)

I confirm I have paid or will pay an amount of Income Tax and/or Capital Gains Tax for each tax year (6 April to 5 April) that is at least equal to the amount of tax that all the charities that I donate to will reclaim on my gifts for that tax year. I understand that other taxes such as VAT or Council Tax do not qualify. I understand the charity will reclaim 25p of tax on every £1 that I give.

☐   My donation does not qualify for Gift Aid.

Signature _____

Date _____

Notes:

1. Please notify BRF if you want to cancel this declaration, change your name or home address, or no longer pay sufficient tax on your income and/or capital gains.

2. If you pay Income Tax at the higher/additional rate and want to receive the additional tax relief due to you, you must include all your Gift Aid donations on your Self-Assessment tax return or ask HM Revenue and Customs to adjust your tax code.

ND0115

BRF PUBLICATIONS ORDER FORM

Please send me the following book(s):

		Quantity	Price	Total
713 6	Barnabas Family Bible (M. Payne & J. Butcher)	___	£9.99	___
245 9	Creative Ideas for Lent & Easter (J. Tibbs)	___	£8.99	___
323 4	Living Liturgies (C. George)	___	£7.99	___
717 4	Messy Easter (J. Leadbetter)	___	£5.99	___
305 0	Messy Family Fun (L. Moore)	___	£9.99	___
3556 0	Reflecting the Glory (T. Wright)	___	£7.99	___
138 4	Ten-Minute Easter Activity Book (B. James)	___	£3.99	___
778 5	Using the Jesus Prayer (J. Twisleton)	___	£6.99	___
010 3	Walking with Gospel Women (F. Stratta)	___	£7.99	___
718 1	Walking with Old Testament Women (F. Stratta)	___	£7.99	___

Total cost of books £ _____
Donation £ _____
Postage and packing £ _____
TOTAL £ _____

POSTAGE AND PACKING CHARGES				
order value	UK	Europe	Surface	Air Mail
£7.00 & under	£1.25	£3.00	£3.50	£5.50
£7.01–£30.00	£2.25	£5.50	£6.50	£10.00
Over £30.00	free	prices on request		

Please complete the payment details below and send with payment to: **BRF, 15 The Chambers, Vineyard, Abingdon OX14 3FE**

Name _____

Address _____

_____ Postcode _____

Tel _____ Email _____

Total enclosed £ _____ (cheques should be made payable to 'BRF')

Please charge my Visa ❏ Mastercard ❏ Switch card ❏ with £ _____

Card no: | | | | | | | | | | | | | | | | | |

Expires | | | | Security code | | | |

Issue no (Switch only) | | | |

Signature (essential if paying by credit/Switch) _____

NEW DAYLIGHT INDIVIDUAL SUBSCRIPTIONS

❏ I would like to take out a subscription myself:

Your name _____

Your address _____

_____ Postcode _____

Tel _____ Email _____

Please send *New Daylight* beginning with the May 2015 / September 2015 / January 2016 issue: (delete as applicable)

(please tick box)	UK	Europe/Economy	Standard
NEW DAYLIGHT	❏ £16.35	❏ £24.00	❏ £27.60
NEW DAYLIGHT 3-year sub	❏ £42.75		
NEW DAYLIGHT DELUXE	❏ £20.70	❏ £32.70	❏ £37.95
NEW DAYLIGHT daily email only	❏ £12.90 (UK and overseas)		

Please complete the payment details below and send with appropriate payment to: **BRF, 15 The Chambers, Vineyard, Abingdon OX14 3FE**

Total enclosed £ _____ (cheques should be made payable to 'BRF')

Please charge my Visa ❏ Mastercard ❏ Switch card ❏ with £ _____

Card no: ⬚⬚⬚⬚⬚⬚⬚⬚⬚⬚⬚⬚⬚⬚⬚⬚⬚⬚⬚

Expires ⬚⬚⬚⬚ Security code ⬚⬚⬚

Issue no (Switch only) ⬚⬚⬚⬚

Signature (essential if paying by card) _____

To set up a direct debit, please also complete the form on page 159 and send it to BRF with this form.

BRF is a Registered Charity

NEW DAYLIGHT GIFT SUBSCRIPTIONS

❏ I would like to give a gift subscription (please provide both names and addresses:

Your name _____

Your address _____

_____ Postcode _____

Tel _____ Email _____

Gift subscription name _____

Gift subscription address _____

_____ Postcode _____

Gift message (20 words max. or include your own gift card for the recipient)

_____

_____

Please send *New Daylight* beginning with the May 2015 / September 2015 / January 2016 issue: (delete as applicable)

(please tick box)	UK	Europe/Economy	Standard
NEW DAYLIGHT	❏ £16.35	❏ £24.00	❏ £27.60
NEW DAYLIGHT 3-year sub	❏ £42.75		
NEW DAYLIGHT DELUXE	❏ £20.70	❏ £32.70	❏ £37.95
NEW DAYLIGHT daily email only	❏ £12.90 (UK and overseas)		

Please complete the payment details below and send with appropriate payment to: **BRF, 15 The Chambers, Vineyard, Abingdon OX14 3FE**

Total enclosed £ _____ (cheques should be made payable to 'BRF')

Please charge my Visa ❏ Mastercard ❏ Switch card ❏ with £ _____

Card no: ▢▢▢▢ ▢▢▢▢ ▢▢▢▢ ▢▢▢▢ ▢▢▢▢

Expires ▢▢▢ Security code ▢▢▢

Issue no (Switch only) ▢▢▢

Signature (essential if paying by card) _____

To set up a direct debit, please also complete the form on page 159 and send it to BRF with this form.

DIRECT DEBIT PAYMENTS

Now you can pay for your annual subscription to BRF notes using Direct Debit. You need only give your bank details once, and the payment is made automatically every year until you cancel it. If you would like to pay by Direct Debit, please use the form opposite, entering your BRF account number under 'Reference'.

You are fully covered by the Direct Debit Guarantee:

The Direct Debit Guarantee

- This Guarantee is offered by all banks and building societies that accept instructions to pay Direct Debits.
- If there are any changes to the amount, date or frequency of your Direct Debit, The Bible Reading Fellowship will notify you 10 working days in advance of your account being debited or as otherwise agreed. If you request The Bible Reading Fellowship to collect a payment, confirmation of the amount and date will be given to you at the time of the request.
- If an error is made in the payment of your Direct Debit, by The Bible Reading Fellowship or your bank or building society, you are entitled to a full and immediate refund of the amount paid from your bank or building society.
  - – If you receive a refund you are not entitled to, you must pay it back when The Bible Reading Fellowship asks you to.
- You can cancel a Direct Debit at any time by simply contacting your bank or building society. Written confirmation may be required. Please also notify us.

The Bible Reading Fellowship

Instruction to your bank or building society to pay by Direct Debit

Please fill in the whole form using a ballpoint pen and send to The Bible Reading Fellowship, 15 The Chambers, Vineyard, Abingdon OX14 3FE.

Service User Number: | 5 | 5 | 8 | 2 | 2 | 9 |

Name and full postal address of your bank or building society

To: The Manager	Bank/Building Society
Address	
	Postcode

Name(s) of account holder(s)

Branch sort code

| | | | | | |

Bank/Building Society account number

| | | | | | | | |

Reference

| | | | | | | |

Instruction to your Bank/Building Society

Please pay The Bible Reading Fellowship Direct Debits from the account detailed in this instruction, subject to the safeguards assured by the Direct Debit Guarantee.
I understand that this instruction may remain with The Bible Reading Fellowship and, if so, details will be passed electronically to my bank/building society.

Signature(s)	
Date	

Banks and Building Societies may not accept Direct Debit instructions for some types of account.

A New BluePrint
for Britain
including everybody
in equal measure.
Plenty provision !
All welcome within
reason; and all to a

GOOD PURPOSE,
please.

P.S. My Mum'd be pleased! AHJ

So am I

PEACE